IMAGES
of America

SEATTLE'S
HISTORIC HOTELS

Indian Totem Pole, Seattle.

Mar 21/06

This is a fine country when it don't rain. It rains always. Regards Junger

No. 2026   Lowman & Hanford S. & P. Co., Seattle

HOTEL SEATTLE. This postcard of Pioneer Square in downtown Seattle showing the Hotel Seattle and Indian Totem Pole was mailed in 1905. The Seattle Hotel was built in 1890 from the ashes of the Great Seattle Fire. The handwriting on the card reads, "This is a fine country when it don't rain. It rains always. Regards, Junger." (Author's collection.)

ON THE COVER: THE DENNY—HOTEL WASHINGTON (1890–1906). Seattle once had the leading hotel of the Northwest. The Denny Hotel was built perched atop Denny Hill. The Denny Hotel was never opened and sat vacant for over a decade. James M. Moore bought and renamed it the Hotel Washington, and it was officially opened in 1903. (Courtesy Seattle Municipal Archives 63801.)

IMAGES
of America

SEATTLE'S
HISTORIC HOTELS

Robin Shannon

ARCADIA
PUBLISHING

Published by Arcadia Publishing
Charleston SC, Chicago IL, Portsmouth NH, San Francisco CA

Printed in the United States of America

Library of Congress Control Number: 2009932664

For all general information contact Arcadia Publishing at:
Telephone 843-853-2070
Fax 843-853-0044
E-mail sales@arcadiapublishing.com
For customer service and orders:
Toll-Free 1-888-313-2665

Visit us on the Internet at www.arcadiapublishing.com

To Dad—I will miss your guidance forever.

CONTENTS

ACKNOWLEDGMENTS

Seattle historians come in many variations, and I would like to thank the many places and people that have contributed to this wonderful project. A great gratitude goes to the Mayflower Park Hotel Historical Society; Audrey McCombs, Craig Packer, and Trish Festin are actively saving Mayflower history. Special thanks to Heather Mitchell, public relations coordinator from the Fairmont Olympic Hotel for making history come alive. Grazie (thanks in Italian) to Andrew M. DeDonker, sales account manager, at the Sorrento Hotel and the Hunt Club for literally taking photographs off the walls for me to scan.

Heartfelt thanks go to the many club members of the Pacific Northwest Postcard club, particularly Mark Sundquist; the Seattle Municipal Archives, particularly Jeff Wares; and the Museum of History and Industry, particularly Carolyn Marr. Thanks to the Seattle Public Library and the University of Washington Special Collections (UWSC); to my editor Sarah J. Higginbotham for giving me words of encouragement; to Jeremy, my son, who put up with endless hours of "What are you doing, mom?" (My reply: "Working on my book!") Last but not least, Laurie ValBush, my travel companion and personal editor. These people and organizations have contributed to this book that you may enjoy opening time and time again.

INTRODUCTION

Seattle's first hotel, the Felker House, was built by Capt. Leonard M. Felker on land known as Maynard's Point, which was the southwest corner of South Jackson Street and First Avenue South. Felker had purchased the land from David S. "Doc" Maynard (1808–1873) and brought the prefabricated building around Cape Horn on the brig *Franklin Adams*. The two-story framed structure featuring a huge veranda along the entire front was managed as a hotel, restaurant, and bordello by Mary Conklin, a tart-tongued Irishwoman who earned the nickname "Mother (later Madame) Damnable." She was a good cook with a rough tongue and nasty temper. Years after her death, during a reburial in 1884, Madam Damnable's body was found to have turned to stone and weighed 1,300 pounds. The Felker House burned to the ground in the Great Seattle Fire of 1889, along with 64 city blocks.

The Occidental Hotel, built in 1865, proclaimed itself to be the largest hotel north of San Francisco. John Collins ran away from Ireland when he was 10 years old. In 1857, he arrived in Port Gamble and ran the lathe mill at Port Gamble. He also managed the company's Teekalet Hotel. Collins purchased one-third interest in the Occidental Hotel in September 1865. It was built on the triangle of land formed by Yesler Way, James Street, and Second Avenue.

A few of Seattle's most sensational events involved the Occidental Hotel. First, U.S. president Rutherford B. Hayes visited Seattle in 1880 and celebrated with a banquet at the Occidental. In 1881, two alleged holdup men were lynched from a nearby maple tree. Adelaide Nichols, Bertrand Collins's oldest cousin, remembered running out onto the Occidental's upper balcony to watch "what Seattle apparently regarded as the most spectacular show ever held in town." Another appalling event occurred during the Chinese Riot. John Collins had what was termed "cheap coolie" Chinese laborers working for him. Immediately after the famous Chinese Riot, angry men stormed into the Occidental and demanded that the hotel's Chinese employees be handed over to them. The owner, Collins, normally a mild-mannered man, became enraged and told the rioters that he would shoot anyone who laid a finger on his workers. Collins escorted his Chinese employees from the hotel to his own house across the street. There, he kept them safe in the basement of his house, with his uncle Will Jackling keeping guard with a shotgun. No rioter came to test his aim.

Eventually Collins acquired the other two-thirds of the hotel. In 1884, he razed the first wooden Occidental Hotel and built the second one in its place. The second Occidental Hotel was destroyed in the Great Seattle Fire on June 6, 1889. British writer Rudyard Kipling (1865–1923), after visiting Seattle soon after the fire, wrote, "In the heart of the business quarters there was a horrible black smudge, as though a Hand had come down and rubbed the place smooth. I know now what being wiped out means. The smudge seemed to be about a mile long, and its blackness was relieved by tents in which men were doing business with the wreck of the stock they had saved." In the Occidental's place, the famous Seattle Hotel was built.

In 1876, the Arlington Hotel was built at First Avenue South and Main Street near the Felker Hotel, owned by the well-known O. N. Morse. Pres. Benjamin Harrison stayed here in May 1891. Across the street stood the New England Hotel, a Seattle landmark, owned and operated by Mrs. M. Harmon. On November 24, 1879, the Squire's Opera House, Seattle's first theater, opened on the east side of Commercial Street (First Avenue South), between Washington and Main Streets. The Opera House was not, however, very profitable, and in September 1882, owner Gov. Watson C. Squire reopened the building as the New Brunswick Hotel. The Brunswick was lighted by gas and advertised a bath on every floor.

In his *History of Seattle*, Clarence Bagley writes, "Seattle was the only town in the county in January 1879. There were here then 18 stores of all descriptions; the population of the town had doubled within the last 18 months." He notes that by May 1879, the city featured four hotels: E. C. Eversham's American House on Yesler Way, Louis's Oriental Hotel on Second Avenue North, John Collins and Company's Occidental Hotel, and L. C. Harmon's New England Hotel at the corner of First Avenue South and Main Street.

In 1889, at the time of the Great Seattle Fire, the Denny Hotel was being built on Denny Hill by a group of developers, including Seattle founding father Arthur Denny (1822–1899). Famed New York architect Stanford White had designed the Washington to be six stories high with 100 rooms and 6 acres of terraced lawns. The developers' bickering kept this magnificent hotel closed. On May 5, 1893, the New York Stock Exchange crashed, and the Panic of 1893 halted the events with interiors unfinished, and the Victorian showpiece stood vacant over Seattle for a decade until purchased by James Moore.

The single hotel left after the Great Seattle Fire was the Bellevue, at First Avenue and Battery Street, also known as Bell's Hotel. Builder William Nathaniel Bell (1817–1887) was one of the original members of the Denny party that arrived at Alki on the schooner *Exact* in 1851. When the hotel was built in 1883, it was dubbed "Bell's Folly" because it was so far from downtown. After the fire, the hotel remained fully booked for three months.

The Great Seattle Fire destroyed over a dozen hotels, but within four years there were approximately 63 hotels operating in the Seattle area. The main tourist hotels erected were the Rainier-Grand Hotel, built in 1889 at First Avenue and Marion Street, and the Rainier Hotel on Fifth Avenue between Columbia and Marion Streets, built the same year in just 90 days following the Seattle fire. Both hotels featured glorious views. The Rainier, however, was never a financial success as the walk up the hill to it was exhausting. The Rainier was razed around 1910, as was the Rainier-Grand Hotel. By the late 1880s, many workingmen's lodgings and fancy hotels were built close to the railway depot along the west side of First Avenue between Columbia and Cherry Streets.

James A. Moore (1861–1929) bought the Denny Hotel and opened it in 1893 as the Hotel Washington. Teddy Roosevelt was his first guest. The Toonerville trolley clanked its way up the hill to drop off the elite clientele. City engineer R. H. Thompson altered the Seattle landscape by a series of regrades. Seattle could have had San Francisco–like terrain had some of our forefathers not gotten a bit carried away.

By the time the regrades had washed away Denny Hill, the Great Depression was well under way. Gone was the grandiose Hotel Washington, and along came the low-rent district in the flattened Denny Triangle, Belltown, and Denny regrade districts. The hotels that were built quickly after the Great Seattle Fire mostly catered to long-term residents. When the Great Depression came along, it restricted growth for awhile, but as always, Seattle fought back.

One

SEATTLE'S DENNY AND WASHINGTON HOTELS

Promoted as "The Scenic Hotel of the West," the majestic Denny Hotel offered a sweeping view of Puget Sound and the snowcapped Cascade and Olympic mountain ranges. Seattle pioneer Arthur Denny (1822–1899) and venture capitalists built the Denny Hotel, but both squabbling between investors and the Panic of 1893 halted its opening. The Denny was built in 1888–1889 at a cost of $500,000, but it sat vacant for a decade, a shell looming over Seattle.

No streets led to the hotel, but the shortest counterbalanced cable car line in the world carried the guests and luggage up 200 feet to the grand entrance. The Denny was six stories high with 100 rooms and 6 acres of lawn. New York architect Stanford White designed the Victorian Gothic hotel, decorating it with massive furniture, oriental rugs, ornate square pillars, and detailed wood paneling.

James M. Moore bought the shell of the Denny Hotel and renamed it the Hotel Washington, opening to the fanfare of Teddy Roosevelt in May 1903. The grand hotel prospered for one or two summers, but Seattle was in the midst of a huge regrade project. Moore and Seattle city engineer Reginald Thompson first met in the spring of 1903. The energetic, forceful Moore and the iron-willed Thompson clashed over Thompson's idea of sluicing Second Avenue and Virginia Street. Eventually persuaded by Thompson's persistence and skyrocketing land prices, Moore came around to the engineer's way of thinking: the Gothic landmark Hotel Washington closed in 1906. A year later, it was washed away into history by the Denny regrade.

The New Hotel Washington opened in 1908 at the corner of Second Avenue and Stewart Street. It stood 13 stories high, featured 275 guest rooms, and had cost J. E. Chiliberg and J. C. Marmaduke's New Washington Improvement Company some $1.8 million to build. Just 27 years later, Marmaduke and his stockholders sold the building for $700,000 to Western Hotels, Inc. In 1963, the New Washington was bought by the Catholic Church, who reopened it as a retirement home, renamed the Josephinum.

HOTEL WASHINGTON. During its short lifetime, the Hotel Washington was also widely known by its original name, the Denny Hotel. The hotel was designed by architect Stanford White of New York. White's design principles embodied the American Renaissance. In 1906, White's murder by fellow millionaire Harry Thaw was touted by Hearst newspapers as "The Crime of the Century." Predictably, it was over a woman: Evelyn Marshall Nesbit, a chorus girl from the show *Florodora*. Nesbit became Thaw's wife and alleged she was a teenage victim of the married White's lechery. Thaw shot White in the face three times at point blank range at Madison Square Garden. The first trial ended in a hung jury. With the tearful Nesbit testifying on his behalf and the best lawyers money could buy, Thaw was declared insane after the second murder trial. Nine years later, he was pronounced cured and released from custody. Evelyn Marshall Nesbit became known as "The Girl in the Red Velvet Swing." (Courtesy UWSC Hamilton 176.)

THE HOTEL WASHINGTON (1890–1906). This 1903 postcard shows the Hotel Washington. This landmark seemed cursed as the developers, including pioneer Arthur Denny, argued amongst themselves, keeping this Victorian hotel dark, empty, and closed. The crash of the New York Stock Market in 1893 helped keep it closed for a decade. Shown here in 1903, it had a short life. (Courtesy Evelyn Marshall.)

HOTEL WASHINGTON ATOP DENNY HILL. This c. 1900 Webster and Stevens photograph looks north at the hotel from Seneca Street. The Plymouth Church is on the right. (Courtesy Seattle Public Library 22943.)

HOTEL WASHINGTON GRAND LOBBY, 1903. The Hotel Washington sat impressively atop Denny Hill between Second and Fourth Avenues and Stewart and Virginia Streets. The elegant building survived only until 1907, when the western part of Denny Hill was leveled by the massive regrading. (Courtesy Seattle Public Library 15233.)

The Old Hotel Washington in 1906. The Hill shown was 200 feet above the present street level, to realize the change see post card 3058.

HOTEL WASHINGTON. This 1906 real photograph postcard shows the doomed old Hotel Washington 200 feet above Seattle's street level on Denny Hill. Seattle's regrading project was one of the most amazing engineering feats accomplished by any city in U.S. history. (Courtesy Evelyn Marshall.)

HOTEL WASHINGTON, 1906   HOTEL WASHINGTON, 1908   WASHINGTON ANNEX

OPEN   *The* REX PHARMACY   FREE MESSENGER
ALL   DUDLEY GREEN, Prop.   SERVICE
NIGHT   Second and Stewart, Seattle   USE YOUR PHONE

POSTCARD OF HOTEL WASHINGTON. This advertisement postcard from the Rex Pharmacy shows the original Hotel Washington atop Denny Hill in 1906, the New Hotel Washington in 1908, and the Hotel Washington Annex. Gone is the majestic architecture of the original Washington to make way for the "absolutely fireproof" steel, granite, brick, and terra-cotta of the New Hotel Washington. (Courtesy Kent and Sandy Renshaw.)

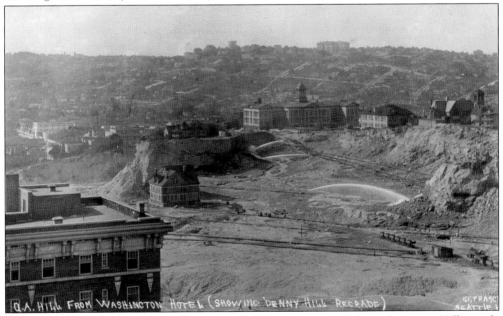

VIEW FROM HOTEL WASHINGTON. This postcard of Queen Anne Hill shows the Denny Hill regrade as seen from the Hotel Washington. Other massive Seattle regrades were the Jackson Hill and the Dearborn Street regrades, which created Harbor Island in 1909. At the time, Harbor Island was the largest artificial island in the world at approximately 350 acres. (Courtesy Mark Sundquist.)

DENNY HILL REGRADE. This Seattle Engineering Department photograph snapped on November 6, 1929 shows how the city sluiced more than 5 million cubic yards of dirt, mostly into Elliott Bay. Some of the buildings in the background are D. N. and E. Walter and Company, the Camlin Hotel, Western Auto Supply, the Vance Hotel, the Hotel Benjamin Franklin, Whitman Furniture Company, and the Sheridan Apartments. (Courtesy Seattle Municipal Archives 3713.)

LEVELING SITE OF HOTEL WASHINGTON. The amount of soil removed during the Seattle upgrade, it is said, was equal to roughly 13 percent of that removed in the digging of the Panama Canal. On January 6, 1899, the first phase of the Denny Hill regrade was finished. On August 29, 1903, C. J. Erickson won a contract to further regrade the hill. This second phase took eight years to complete. (Author's collection.)

14

Second Ave. North from Pine St., Seattle, Washington

NEW WASHINGTON AND WASHINGTON ANNEX. This postcard view of Second Avenue North from Pine Street shows the Hotel Washington Annex with the New Hotel Washington just beyond it. The New Hotel Washington was built on land in front of the old Hotel Washington. The Denny Hill regrade can be seen on the right in this postcard. (Author's collection.)

The NEW WASHINGTON HOTEL, Seattle, Wash.

THE NEW HOTEL WASHINGTON. A small pamphlet put out by the New Hotel Washington boasted, "Each room at the New Hotel Washington is an outside room. No matter what direction your windows face—the view is beautiful. Every room is cheerfully and tastefully furnished. Every room has a bath." (Courtesy Kent and Sandy Renshaw.)

15

"Finest in the Northwest." The back of this postcard states, "The New Washington is Seattle's largest fashionable hotel, the finest in the Northwest. It is however, but one of many of the elegant hostelries in the City." The Washington advertised the European plan at reasonable rates. In 1954, the Colonel's Corner restaurant had a Deep South plantation theme. (Courtesy Mark Sundquist.)

Main Dining Room. This postcard shows the New Washington Hotel's main dining room. In the 1930s, Western Hotels acquired the New Washington Hotel and used the hotel as its headquarters. In 1955, Western Hotels sold the New Washington for more than $1 million and moved its home offices to its Olympic Hotel. (Author's collection.)

Main Dining Room, New Washington Hotel, Seattle, Wash.

NEW HOTEL WASHINGTON MENU. This Coffee Shop menu from the New Hotel Washington offers 10¢ coffee and 15¢ western beer. Though 10¢ coffee may have seemed expensive to some hotel guests, a full-course breakfast including an entree, juice, coffee, and a Danish or toast was only 45¢–95¢. (Author's collection.)

NEW HOTEL WASHINGTON MENU INSIDE. This Coffee Shop menu offered breakfast, lunch, and dinner. This photograph shows the Coffee Shop club breakfasts on the left and the a la carte menu on the right. An additional charge of 20¢ per person was charged for room service. (Author's collection.)

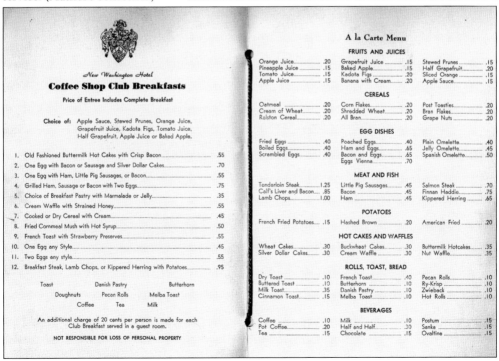

New Washington Hotel

Coffee Shop Club Breakfasts

Price of Entree Includes Complete Breakfast

Choice of: Apple Sauce, Stewed Prunes, Orange Juice, Grapefruit Juice, Kadota Figs, Tomato Juice, Half Grapefruit, Apple Juice or Baked Apple.

1. Old Fashioned Buttermilk Hot Cakes with Crisp Bacon	.55
2. One Egg with Bacon or Sausage and Silver Dollar Cakes	.70
3. One Egg with Ham, Little Pig Sausages, or Bacon	.55
4. Grilled Ham, Sausage or Bacon with Two Eggs	.75
5. Choice of Breakfast Pastry with Marmalade or Jelly	.35
6. Cream Waffle with Strained Honey	.55
7. Cooked or Dry Cereal with Cream	.45
8. Fried Cornmeal Mush with Hot Syrup	.50
9. French Toast with Strawberry Preserves	.55
10. One Egg any Style	.45
11. Two Eggs any style	.55
12. Breakfast Steak, Lamb Chops, or Kippered Herring with Potatoes	.95

Toast	Danish Pastry	Butterhorn
Doughnuts	Pecan Rolls	Melba Toast
	Coffee Tea Milk	

An additional charge of 20 cents per person is made for each Club Breakfast served in a guest room.

NOT RESPONSIBLE FOR LOSS OF PERSONAL PROPERTY

A la Carte Menu

FRUITS AND JUICES

Orange Juice	.20	Grapefruit Juice	.15	Stewed Prunes	.15
Pineapple Juice	.15	Baked Apple	.15	Half Grapefruit	.20
Tomato Juice	.15	Kadota Figs	.20	Sliced Orange	.15
Apple Juice	.15	Banana with Cream	.20	Apple Sauce	.15

CEREALS

Oatmeal	.20	Corn Flakes	.20	Post Toasties	.20
Cream of Wheat	.20	Shredded Wheat	.20	Bran Flakes	.20
Ralston Cereal	.20	All Bran	.20	Grape Nuts	.20

EGG DISHES

Fried Eggs	.40	Poached Eggs	.40	Plain Omelette	.40
Boiled Eggs	.40	Ham and Eggs	.65	Jelly Omelette	.45
Scrambled Eggs	.40	Bacon and Eggs	.65	Spanish Omelette	.50
		Eggs Vienna	.70		

MEAT AND FISH

Tenderloin Steak	1.25	Little Pig Sausages	.45	Salmon Steak	.70
Calf's Liver and Bacon	.85	Bacon	.45	Finnan Haddie	.75
Lamb Chops	1.00	Ham	.45	Kippered Herring	.65

POTATOES

French Fried Potatoes	.15	Hashed Brown	.20	American Fried	.20

HOT CAKES AND WAFFLES

Wheat Cakes	.30	Buckwheat Cakes	.30	Buttermilk Hotcakes	.35
Silver Dollar Cakes	.30	Cream Waffle	.30	Nut Waffle	.35

ROLLS, TOAST, BREAD

Dry Toast	.10	French Toast	.40	Pecan Rolls	.10
Buttered Toast	.10	Butterhorn	.10	Ry-Krisp	.10
Milk Toast	.35	Danish Pastry	.10	Zwieback	.10
Cinnamon Toast	.15	Melba Toast	.10	Hot Rolls	.10

BEVERAGES

Coffee	.10	Milk	.10	Postum	.15
Pot Coffee	.20	Half and Half	.30	Sanka	.15
Tea	.15	Chocolate	.15	Ovaltine	.15

SEATTLE AT NIGHT FROM ROOF. This is a dramatic, moonlit view of Seattle from the New Washington Hotel roof garden. This view looks down Second Avenue towards the east, showing Mount Rainier and the Smith Tower. (Courtesy Mark Sundquist.)

READING AND WRITING ROOM. This postcard of the Reading and Writing Room at the Hotel Washington is dated July 26, 1910. A hotel brochure stated, "The magnificent lobbies—the spacious corridors—the finely furnished parlors—testify to a taste in decoration that makes one understand why the New Washington Hotel is appreciated by persons of culture as a real home." (Author's collection.)

LOBBY OF NEW WASHINGTON HOTEL. Depicted here is a *c.* 1910 postcard showing businessmen in the main lobby of the New Washington Hotel. The Washington had every gadget and convenience the ingenuity of the best architects could devise. Alaska marble was used extensively in the new lobby. (Author's collection.)

SECTION OF LOBBY. This postcard shows a section of the lobby of the New Washington Hotel. The decorating theme included sleek modern leather chairs, antique oriental rugs, soft frosted globes of light, and elaborate square marble pillars holding up huge carved beams along the high ceilings. (Courtesy Kent and Sandy Renshaw.)

THE NEW
WASHINGTON HOTEL
SEATTLE

K.P. BARR NOTE CO. SEATTLE

BROCHURE FOR NEW WASHINGTON HOTEL. Several Seattle hotels advertised their hostelries in small brochures such as this one. This New Washington leaflet included photographs of the reception room, main lobby, main dining room, roof garden, foyer, and the scenic view of the Seattle waterfront from across Elliott Bay. (Author's collection.)

ROOF GARDEN

Each room at the New Washington Hotel is an outside room. No matter in what direction your windows face—the view is beautiful. Every room is cheerfully and tastefully furnished. Every room has a bath.
Built of steel, granite, brick and terra cotta, the New Washington is absolutely fire proof. The same care exercised in preparing to minister to the creature comforts of its guests was shown in the heavier construction of the building itself.

ROOF GARDEN. The brochure included this photograph of the hotel's roof garden. One-half of the roof gardens were enclosed in glass. Pres. Theodore Roosevelt, Pres. William Howard Taft, Pres. Woodrow Wilson, Pres. Warren G. Harding, and then vice president Calvin Coolidge might have relaxed on the rooftop garden. (Author's collection.)

BABE RUTH AT THE WASHINGTON HOTEL. This c. 1927 photograph shows baseball great Babe Ruth (1895–1948) surrounded by young children at the bottom of a staircase being fed a turkey leg by a boy. The stairs belong to the New Hotel Washington; the hotel manager's son Harold Warner is the fair-haired boy standing on the stairs just above Babe Ruth. (Courtesy MOHAI 1986.5G.2634.)

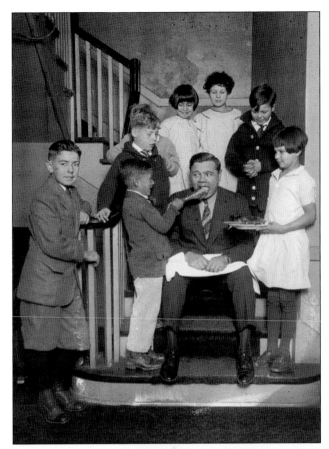

MEZZANINE FLOOR. This postcard shows the mezzanine of the New Washington Hotel. Several national organizations have held conventions at the hotel, including the U.S. Chamber of Commerce, the Shriners, the American Bankers, and the American Bar Association. Nobility stayed at the hotel during the Alaska-Yukon-Pacific Exposition in 1909. (Courtesy Kent and Sandy Renshaw.)

Mezzanine Floor, New Washington Hotel, Seattle, U. S. A.

SECTION OF LOBBY, HOTEL WASHINGTON, SEATTLE, U. S. A.

TOTEM FIRE PLACE
HOTEL WASHINGTON.
SEATTLE.

ROMANS PHOTO CO
SEATTLE.

TOTEM POLE ROOM. Author Kate C. Duncan writes that the hotel lobby's mantle, totem poles, and the tile murals above and to the sides were made in 1907 or 1908 by Rookwood Pottery of Cincinnati, Ohio. Ye Olde Curiosity Shop provided the totem poles that Rookwood used as models. (Courtesy Kent and Sandy Renshaw.)

TOTEM FIREPLACE. This 1908 photograph postcard by Romans Photo shows a close-up of the Hotel Washington's famous totem fireplace (with a $1,250 price tag). The totem pole on the left is modeled after the Seattle totem pole, and the one on the right is a replica of the Chief Shakes pole at Wrangell, Alaska. (Courtesy Dan Kerlee.)

NEW HOTEL WASHINGTON. This photograph postcard shows the Moore Theater on the left, the New Hotel Washington at center, and the New Washington Annex on the right. The New Hotel Washington, built by James Crawford Marmaduke and stockholders, sold for $700,000 in 1937. In 1907–1908, the original investment of the furnishings and real estate was more than $1.8 million. (Courtesy John Cooper.)

HOTEL WASHINGTON ANNEX. Next to the Hotel Washington was the hotel's annex, located on the corner of Second Avenue and Stewart Street. The rates were $1 a night and up, and the hotel offered attractive rates for "permanent guests." G. Henry Whitcomb in 1905–1906 bought all of the property on the east side of Second Avenue from Pine to Stewart Avenues and built the Hotel Washington Annex. (Courtesy Kent and Sandy Renshaw.)

HOTEL WASHINGTON ANNEX

Seattle

LOBBY, HOTEL WASHINGTON ANNEX. A hotel advertisement read, "Hotel Washington Annex is ideally located for those who wish to be in easy touch with the activities of the city, though it is sufficiently removed from the turmoil and dirt of the proverbial down-town hotel." (Courtesy Kent and Sandy Renshaw.)

RECEPTION ROOM, HOTEL WASHINGTON ANNEX. Billed as a place "Where Comfort Eases and Service Pleases," this social room was in keeping with the hominess of the rooms and suites. The fireplace was surrounded by easy chairs, divans, and a piano in a setting of elegant leisure. (Courtesy Evelyn Marshall.)

VIEW FROM NEW WASHINGTON HOTEL. This December 1, 1928, photograph shows Second Avenue lights from the Washington Hotel, looking south. Visible is the sign for the Hotel Gowman, which had been the Hotel Washington Annex. In later years, the New Washington featured the popular Casbah supper club. (Courtesy Seattle Municipal Archives 3188.)

GOWMAN HOTEL. The Hotel Washington Annex later became the Gowman Hotel and finally the Stewart Hotel before its demolition. The Gowman Hotel advertised itself as "The Hotel with a Personality." (Courtesy Alan Peterson.)

The HOTEL GOWMAN ~ Sea

The Hotel With A Personality

A glimpse of The Gowman's Main Dining room.

AROUND this famous Seattle hostelry there has grown to be an atmosphere and tradition of hospitality—based in part upon the cordial friendliness of "Mine Host" Gowman and his efficient corps of assistants and in part upon the class of guests which this attracts.

The Hotel Gowman is one which seasoned travelers mention when discussing the places where they like to stop—one where the stranger to the city feels "at home" immediately—one where almost any guest is likely to find friends and acquaintances or make them if he so desires.

In equipment and service, those material qualities which

are essential to the preservation of this fine spirit, The Gowman is entitled to rank as a "first class" hotel. Of fireproof construction, modern in every respect (all outside rooms), located in the heart of Seattle's shopping and theater district, it offers every desirable convenience to its guests. The rooms are newly and most comfortably furnished, the lobby, parlor and other public accommodations are inviting to the point of luxuriousness.

The dining rooms and coffee shop have a well deserved reputation for the excellence of the meals and the service. Many organizations, clubs and societies choose The Gowman as a place for their banquets and social functions.

Written or wired reservations will receive prompt attention, that your sojourn in Seattle may be most enjoyable.

The Creed of
MINE HOST GOWMAN

To greet you—as in days of yore,
   The Host received you at his door
With courteous formality,
   To proffer hospitality,
That springs sincerely from the heart,
   To play ye olde time landlord's part,
In studying your every need,
   Yet not obtrude in word or deed.
To earn of you this simple boast:
   "He was in very truth MINE
   HOST!"

Managing Director.

HOTEL GOWMAN BROCHURE. A poem from the brochure reads: "The Creed of MINE HOST GOWMAN—To greet you—as in days of yore, The Host received you at his door, With courteous formality, To proffer hospitality, That springs sincerely from the heart. To play ye olde time landlord's part, In studying your every need, Yet not obtrude in word or deed. To earn of you this simple boast: 'He was in very truth MINE HOST!' T. H. Gowman, Managing Director." (Author's collection.)

INSIGNIA OF THE U.S. ARMED FORCES

ARMY

NAVY

MARINES

HOTEL GOWMAN

Second and Stewart   SEATTLE, WASHINGTON

"The Hotel with a Personality"

T. HARRY GOWMAN, Managing Director

HOTEL GOWMAN MENU FRONT COVER. This menu from the Hotel Gowman dates to 1943. The front and back of the wartime menu feature insignias of the U.S. armed forces. T. Harry Gowman was the hotel's managing director. (Author's collection.)

HOTEL GOWMAN MENU BACK COVER. The back of the same 1943 menu shows officers' collar insignias. Several clubs, societies, and organizations choose the Gowman as a place for their social functions and banquets. At the hotel, a Puget Sound dinner cost $1.25 and included crab leg cocktail; soup; a dinner salad; an extra cut of salmon or halibut or Willapa oysters; and dessert with coffee. (Author's collection.)

HOTEL GOWMAN

Thursday, April 29, 1943

SELECTIVE DINNERS
(Served from 5 P.M. to 9 P.M.)

Choice of One:
    Crab Meat Cocktail   Fruit Cocktail
             Chilled Apple Juice
             Vegetable Soup
             Dinner Salad

Plate of Vegetables	.85
Deviled Crab Meat in Pattie Shell	.85
Pork Chop Casserole with Dressing	.90
Grilled Fresh Halibut Steak, Maitre d'Hotel	1.00
French Fried Scallops, Lemon	1.10
Roast Stuffed Half Spring Chicken, Pan Gravy	1.40
Grilled Rainbow Trout	*1.00*

Lemon Pie   Deep Dish Apple Cobbler
Caramel Sundae   Baked Custard
Jello with Whipped Cream   Layer Cake

Coffee   Milk   Tea

PUGET SOUND DINNER 1.25

Crab Leg or ~~Shrimp Cocktail~~

Soup du Jour   Dinner Salad

Extra Cut of Salmon Steak
Extra Cut of Halibut Steak
Fried Willapoint Oysters
Vegetable   Potatoes
Choice of Dessert
Coffee, Tea or Milk

The Management of this Hotel assures it's patrons that all foods served here are bought from recognized and reputable sources. We will not tolerate any dealings with the black market.
                                The Gowman

(Booth and Table Minimum Service Charge 50¢ Thru Dinner Hour)

HOTEL GOWMAN MENU INSIDE. During the height of wartime rationing, the hotel's management assured its patrons, "all foods served here are bought from recognized and reputable sources. We will not tolerate any dealings with the black market, The Gowman." Dinners included crab cocktail, chilled apple juice, dinner salad, choice of entree (such as fresh Rainbow trout), and lemon pie for 85¢–$1.40. (Author's collection.)

REGRADE CHANGES. This postcard shows the regrade changes in Seattle from 1906 to 1908. The top portion of this postcard shows the original Washington Hotel atop Denny Hill before the 1906 regrade. Overzealous regrading washed Denny Hill into the sound. Seattle city engineer R. H. Thompson thought if Denny Hill were flattened then horse-drawn streetcars and development of the Seattle downtown would flourish north of the city. The bottom portion of this postcard shows the New Washington Hotel in 1908, after the regrade. Located next to the New Washington Hotel is the Hotel Washington Annex. Soon after Denny Hill was regraded, the horse-drawn streetcars for whom it was leveled were replaced by automobiles. Belltown and the regrade area became a blue-collar district with taverns, parking lots, automobile dealerships, and a few apartments and hotels. (Courtesy Mark Sundquist.)

Two

SIMPLY ONE OF A KIND: THE MAYFLOWER HOTEL

To step into the historic Mayflower Park Hotel today is to be transformed back to a time of elegance and Old World charm. Watch the tourists stroll by while sipping a classic martini with "drunken olives," or stay in one of the beautifully appointed guest rooms. This historic hotel has had several lives since its July 16, 1927, opening as the Bergonian Hotel. Located at 405 Olive Way, what would become today's Mayflower Park Hotel was designed by Stuart and Wheatley Architects and engineers Fred Bassetti and Company for owner-operator Stephen Berg.

The Bergonian—named, according to Berg's son, after the *Oregonian*—was soon ranked as one of the finest hotels in Seattle. Berg had a reputation as a pioneer uptown hotel builder and his 12-story tourist hotel included 211 guest rooms (all with baths), several retail shops, a barbershop, formal dining room, and a café/coffee shop. The Bergonian's initial cost was $750,000, and builders used distinctive terra-cotta materials designed in the Italian Renaissance architecture. Unfortunately, during the crash of 1929, Berg lost everything and eventually declared bankruptcy.

The Fourth and Olive Corporation redeemed the Bergonian from foreclosure in 1933 and during Western Hotels's management from 1933 to 1955. In 1933, the Bergonian Hotel was remodeled and its name was changed to Mayflower Hotel. When a 1948 change in liquor laws finally allowed the selling of liquor by the drink, the Mayflower opened the Carousel Room in 1949, the first hotel cocktail lounge in Seattle.

Sadly neglected from 1961 to 1974, this landmark went through numerous bankruptcies and in 1974 was purchased by its current owners, Birney and Marie Dempcy, along with a small group of partners. The newly renamed Mayflower Park Hotel has been lovingly restored to its historic magnificence. In 1976, blue laws prohibiting minors from viewing preparation of mixed drinks was lifted just prior to the opening of Oliver's Lounge, making it the state's first daylight bar.

The Mayflower Park Hotel is listed in Historic Hotels of America, and yes, as the hotel's promotional materials claim, it is, quite simply, one of a kind.

BERGONIAN HOTEL CONSTRUCTION. This photograph taken in 1926 shows the Bergonian Hotel construction at Fourth Avenue and Olive Street. Marie Dempcy, one of the hotel's current owners, says the Mayflower Park Hotel has a friendly ghost. She says, "We think he is the spirit of an elderly gentlemen who occupied an apartment on the sixth floor for years." (Courtesy MOHAI 1983.10.697.)

BERGONIAN HOTEL. On July 16, 1927, the Bergonian Hotel officially opened. On that date the *Hotel News of the West* quoted a Bergonian staff member named Thompson as declaring, "We are out after the Davenport's reputation. No one has been employed who can't smile, and we want to give the type of service which will make everybody feel at home." (Courtesy MOHAI 1983.10.3591.)

MAYFLOWER HOTEL. When the Bergonian Hotel was built during the prosperous 1920s, the neighborhood's original residential district was destroyed to make way for the high-rise commercial buildings. The Campbell Sign Company designed and installed the Mayflower sign. (Courtesy Alan Peterson.)

VIEW FROM MAYFLOWER HOTEL. Here is a 1935 photograph taken from the window of the Mayflower Hotel. Charles W. Hunlock to date holds the record for longest tenure as general manager at the hotel, having held the post for 13 years. (Author's collection.)

JACK AND JILL GRILL. On March 13, 1933, the *Hotel News of the West* reported, "More than 1,200 persons attended the invitational preview inspection of the new Jack and Jill Grill and Terrace Dining Room at the Seattle Bergonian Hotel Tuesday. . . . The Mother Goose rhyme of "Jack and Jill" is depicted in gayly painted scenes on the walls of the grill and are from the talented brush of Franz Zallinger." The former Jack and Jill Grill later became the coffee shop and is currently the Andaluca Restaurant. (Courtesy MOHAI 1983.10.13656.2.)

MAYFLOWER HOTEL UPPER LOBBY. A grand staircase with wrought-iron handrails connects the lower and upper lobbies. Leaded stained-glass windows with fleur-de-lys (flowers of the lily) and a "B" inscription representing the original hotel name, Bergonian, still allow subtle light into the lobby. Gone are the murals on the walls, but the unique fireplace is still there. Notice the barbershop sign on the lower left—it too has vanished. (Courtesy MOHAI 1983.10.13679.)

MAYFLOWER HOTEL INTERIOR. According to the *Hotel News of the West,* February 1934, "The Hotel Mayflower, until recently the Bergonian, is rapidly undergoing a transformation and will soon present a complete new appearance. The lobby has been completely rearranged, redecorated, and will be re-carpeted and refurnished as soon as the alterations are completed. The Front Office Desk has been moved opposite the elevators, where the cigar stand was, which has been moved to the opposite side of the entrance." This photograph, taken by Webster and Stevens in 1936, shows the makeover of the lower lobby at the Mayflower Hotel. (Courtesy MOHAI 1983.10.13656.1.)

COFFEE SHOP, 1938. *Hotel News of the West* reported the following in March 1938: "A comprehensive program of redecorating and modernizing the coffee shop of the Mayflower Hotel in Seattle has just recently been completed, and the results of this brightening have brought many compliments to Charles W. Hunlock, manager." The coffee shop is presently the Andaluca Restaurant. (Courtesy MOHAI 1983.10.13838.1.)

STOCK CERTIFICATE. The Hotel Mayflower Company issued "exactly one shares exactly" to Edmond S. Meany Jr. on January 22, 1934. A year later, Meany died of a stroke in Denny Hall on the University of Washington campus, just before he was to give a lecture on Canadian history. (Courtesy Mayflower Park Hotel.)

CAROUSEL ROOM MENU. The Carousel Room was decorated in bright circus colors with carousel horses suspended from the ceiling. A quote from the back of the Carousel Room menu, reads, "With the world so intent on getting somewhere it is relaxing to just whirl musically around and get nowhere at all." The Carousel Room is now Oliver's Lounge. (Courtesy Mayflower Park Hotel.)

CAROUSEL ROOM MENU INSIDE. A Rob Roy, Side Car, and a Stinger were each 85¢, and a Carnival Cooler was a mere $1.10. Manager George Marble had converted the former Polka Dot Shop into the intimate Carousel Room. Female shoppers were the lounge's best customers. (Courtesy Mayflower Park Hotel.)

Menu

DINNER

DUNGENESS CRAB COCKTAIL . . . . 1.45   JUMBO SHRIMP COCKTAIL 1.45
With Our Own Special Dressing

TOSSED GREEN SALAD, CAROUSEL DRESSING 90

From the Charcoal Broiler

NEW YORK STEAK, Premium Choice . . 4.95   **CHOICE TOP SIRLOIN,** Eastern Steer . . 4.50
DEEP FRIED PRAWNS . . . . 3.00   DEEP FRIED CRAB LEGS 3.25
Two Superb Sauces
Silver Foil Wrapped Baked Potato or French Fried Potatoes

Chef's Special Dinner	**Sandwiches**		**Ladies' Steak**
CHARCOAL-BROILED CHOPPED SIRLOIN STEAK — Tossed Green Salad Long Branch Potatoes Hot Garlic Roll 2.45	PAUL BUNYAN HAMBURGER SANDWICH Long Branch Potatoes TOSSED GREEN SALAD 1.90	CHARCOAL-BROILED TOP SIRLOIN STEAK SANDWICH Long Branch Potatoes TOSSED GREEN SALAD 2.15	SELECT SIRLOIN STEAK *with "Carousel Butter Supreme"* Foil Wrapped Baked Potato or Long Branch Potatoes Hot Garlic Roll 3.50

TEA, COFFEE or MILK 15

Rob Roy 85
Side Car 85
Stinger 85

liqueurs
Benedictine 95
B. & B. 95

CARNIVAL COOLER . . . 1.10

highballs
Bar Bourbon 60
Bonded Whiskies 90
Canadian Whiskies 80
Bar Scotch 85

Suggests for your
FRESH CRAB
Hard Roll

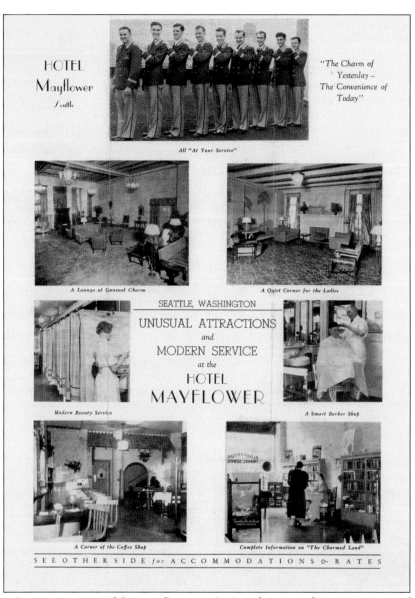

UNUSUAL ATTRACTIONS AND MODERN SERVICE. Among the unusual attractions near the Hotel Mayflower might be Ye Olde Curiosity Shop or Bill Speidel's Underground Tour. There are two lounges depicted here: a lounge of unusual charm and a quiet corner for the ladies upstairs. The July 1957 edition of *Hotel News of the West* reported on the Mayflower's battle against minimum wage in an article titled, "5 Reasons why Nation's Hotels should be Exempt from Increases by Federal Wage and Hour Law." The reasons were as follows: "1. Not factory with 8-10 hour days but a 24-hour business. 2. Purely intrastate—producing no goods. 3. Impossible to interpolate into cash wage fringe issues, such as meals, lodgings, uniforms, tips, etc. 4. Pride on engaging elderly, young, housewives, seasonal employees, and unskilled workers. If hotels were obliged to pay a minimum of $1/hour or more, this type of worker would be discharged immediately and become possibly unemployable. 5. Aggravate the competitive situation with the 100+ employer having to comply and the less than 100 staying exempt—putting the burden on the larger hotels." (Courtesy Mayflower Park Hotel.)

OLIVER'S LOUNGE. The corner of the hotel that houses Oliver's Lounge was originally occupied by one of the city's first Bartell Drug Stores. In 1933, Western Hotels International (Westin) bought the hotel and put in the windowless Carousel Room. In 1976, Oliver's Lounge opened and is still renowned for its International Martini Classic Challenge. (Courtesy Mayflower Park Hotel.)

MAYFLOWER HOTEL, 1939. This photograph taken on March, 29, 1939, in downtown Seattle shows many signs, including Tilton's, Burnett Brothers Jewelers, Gasco, Colonial Theatre, Bigelow Building, Spring's Restaurant, Hotel Mayflower, and the Hotel Ritz. A large (overall dimension of 52 by 35 feet) double-faced "Hotel Mayflower" sign was placed on the rooftop in 1937. The red letters were 8 feet high. (Courtesy Seattle Municipal Archives 38853.)

THE SEATTLE GREETER. This guide to Seattle was offered at Seattle hotels in June 1954. Allan Pomeroy, Seattle's mayor, wrote, "Welcome to Seattle—and welcome to all the Puget Sound country. The hospitality and friendliness of this Northwest corner of the U.S.A. are traditional. May your stay be as pleasant as you could wish. Your host will gladly help you with suggestions for visiting our sister cities of Puget Sound and their many fine attractions." The cover picture on this booklet was of his Royal Highness, the Duke of Edinburgh, who was representing the Queen of England at the spectacular British Empire Games in nearby Vancouver, British Columbia, from July 7 to August 7, 1954. The gathering was the largest in Canadian history to that date and the biggest Empire gathering since the coronation that witnessed over 800 athletes from 25 countries competing in a variety of sporting events. (Author's collection.)

Three

SEATTLE'S GRAND DAME: THE OLYMPIC HOTEL

The Olympic Hotel was completed in 1924 by architects George B. Post and Sons. It was built on 10 acres of land donated to the University of Washington by pioneer families: the Dennys, Landers, and Terrys. In 1895, the university was relocated to the present 583-acre Montlake site and the downtown property was leased to Seattle's Metropolitan Building Company whose subsidiary, Olympic Hotel Corporation, operated the $5.5 million Olympic Hotel. The *Seattle Times* held a contest to name the hotel, and after 3,906 entries, "The Olympic" was chosen.

Two days after the Japanese attack on Pearl Harbor, Victory Square outside the Olympic became Seattle's civic focal point, and it would remain so throughout World War II. Victory Square was home to bond drives, rallies, and eventually a monument that listed the names of Washington State citizens who lost their lives during the war. Victory Square became the Olympic Plaza.

The Metropolitan Theatre was demolished in 1954; the Olympic surrounded the Metropolitan on three sides. In 1955, Westin Hotels bought the Olympic and constructed the Grand Ballroom. In August 1957, the hotel's new drive-in entrance opened, using the space left by the Metropolitan.

The Olympic was registered as a Seattle historical monument and placed on the National Register of Historic Places in 1979. A year later, the Four Seasons Hotels signed a 60-year lease of the Olympic. The grand dame underwent a 20-month, $60 million restoration, one of the largest privately financed historic restorations in U.S. history. In 1982, the Olympic reopened as the Four Seasons Olympic Hotel. Its 756 existing small rooms had been converted into 450 larger guest rooms. In 1984, the Olympic became the first Washington State hotel ever to earn a AAA Five Diamond Award.

During the remodel, an urn of ashes was found in the wall of Shuckers Bar. A couple who met at the Olympic during World War II had wished to become entombed there. Also found was a wall safe hidden behind a painting. A locksmith was summoned to open it; it was empty. Fairmont Hotels and Resorts took over management of the Olympic in August 2003. The new name is now the Fairmont Olympic, but Seattleites still call it "The Olympic."

OLYMPIC HOTEL. The Olympic Hotel was built in 1924 in the Italian Renaissance style. The building surrounded the Metropolitan Theatre and dominated the entire block. The base was made of black Belgian marble and granite. The shops on ground level were decorated in gold and black Italian marble. The Olympic was financed through community gold bonds and built for $4,574,000. (Courtesy John Cooper.)

OLYMPIC LOUNGE. The Olympic Assembly Lounge (now the Spanish Foyer) was near the Fourth Avenue entrance. From the main lobby, an elliptical staircase surrounded by Corinthian columns of American oak led to this magnificent lounge. The lounge led to the Spanish Ballroom, the main ballroom, and the Italian Ballroom. Below the lounge was the Marine Room and five kitchens. (Courtesy John Cooper.)

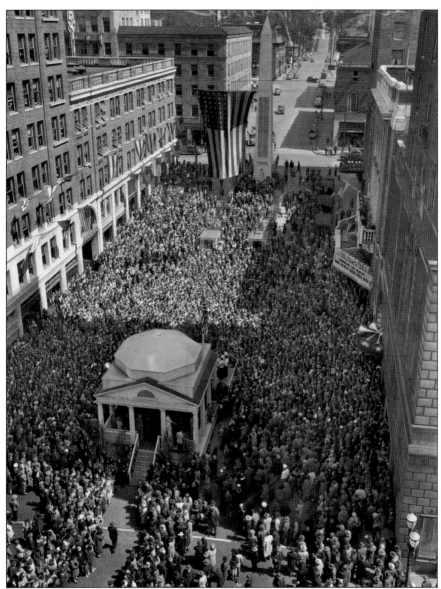

VICTORY SQUARE. Directly in front of the Olympic Hotel, on University Street between Fourth and Fifth Avenues, was the hub of Seattle's home-front activities during World War II. Crowds gathered here at Victory Square for parades, war bond rallies, and many other patriotic events. On June 15, 1942, actress Lana Turner came to Victory Square to promote war bonds. She autographed bond receipts at Victory Square, attended a benefit dance at the Trianon Ballroom, and sold bonds at I. Magnim's department store. Turner promised to kiss anyone who bought a $25,000 bond at the Star Spangled Bond Rally at the Civic Auditorium that evening. The popular movie star attracted the largest crowds seen in the square to that date. Entertainer Bob Hope also spoke to a crowd in Victory Square in 1942 promoting war bonds. After the war, the monument covered in names of soldiers who died in the war from Washington State remained until 1949, but the speaker's stage was torn down almost immediately. Today Benaroya Hall has a Garden of Remembrance memorial that lists the names of Washingtonians who died in military service during World War II. (Courtesy MOHAI PI28279.)

OLYMPIC SPANISH BALLROOM. This is a postcard of the Spanish Ballroom. The ballroom was decorated in tones of fawn, antique gold, and green with elaborate chandeliers and sconces. The Spanish Ballroom was used in the 1977 television movie *Eleanor and Franklin: The White House Years*. Located in the west wing, the Spanish Ballroom is still a popular venue for receptions and weddings. (Courtesy John Cooper.)

OLYMPIC WESTERN HOTEL MARINE ROOM. This 1960s postcard shows the remodeled Marine Room, dubbed "the Snake Pit" by its gay clientele. Gone were the maritime murals by Eric Trumbull. The Marine Room's ship decor also vanished. The Marine Room closed in July 1974 to reopen as a discotheque, The Downstairs, which was itself later renamed the Yellow Submarine Room. (Courtesy Alan Peterson.)

OLYMPIC MARINE ROOM ASHTRAY. Here is a Olympic Hotel Marine Room ashtray produced by Wallace China of Los Angeles. The glaze is white and gloss green. (Author's collection.)

OLYMPIC HOTEL WITH SKYBRIDGE. The printing on the back of the postcard reads: "Olympic Hotel at Fourth and Seneca, Pacific Northwest's finest and most versatile hotel. 800 modern guest rooms and suites. Glass enclosed skybridge connects the hotel to the Olympic garage and Airline terminal for convenient auto and air arrivals. Five restaurants and night spots." The unattractive skybridge was removed in 1985. (Courtesy Mike McCormick.)

GEORGIAN ROOM AT OLYMPIC HOTEL. This photograph shows society women eating at the elegant Georgian Room in 1948. Its linen-covered, silver-and-crystal-set tables have served presidents, entertainers, and royalty. The chic Georgian Room is still open and features French-inspired Northwest cuisine, but without the French girl vending cigarettes and cigars. (Courtesy MOHAI 1986.5.9615.)

THE GEORGIAN ROOM MENU. Around the 1950s, the Georgian Room featured multiple lunch and dinner menus with various covers. On the back of this menu, Tom Gildersleve is listed as the general manager. The Georgian Room was and still is the hotel's main dining room. (Author's collection.)

THE GEORGIAN ROOM LUNCH MENU. Dated Monday, August 22, 1949, this lunch menu stated, "Selective Luncheons. . . The price of the principal item (cold dish, egg, fish, or entree) is the cost of the complete luncheon." Prices ranged from $1.50 for the chef's special luncheon to $2.60 for roast prime ribs of beef au jus. When the hotel remodeled the Georgian Room, blackout paint from World War II had to be chipped off of some of the windows. (Author's collection.)

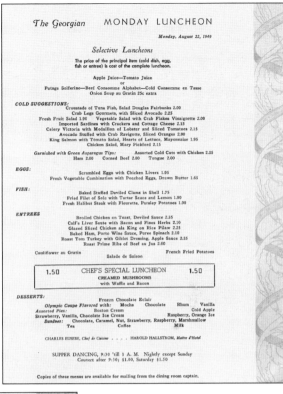

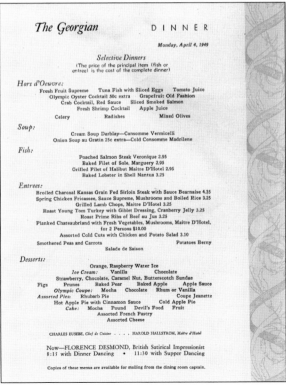

THE GEORGIAN ROOM DINNER MENU. The Georgian dinner on Monday, April 4, 1949, featured hors d'oeuvre, soup, and an entree, including dessert, for a total price (depending on the entree chosen) of between $2.95 and $4.35. Chateaubriand for two was a mere $10. Charles Eusebe was the chef de cuisine and Harold Hallstrom was the maitre d'hotel. (Author's collection.)

OLYMPIC RESTAURANTS AND LOUNGES.
The Marine Room (top) was a Continental dining room with a stylish atmosphere. Clifford and Clark entertained nightly at the Hammond and Steinway. The Olympic Grill (second from top) was a favorite meeting place for breakfast, luncheon, and dinner. It served excellent food at popular prices and had a counter facility for exceptionally fast service. The Terrace Room (third from top) was an informal and intimate cocktail lounge just off the lobby. The hotel advertised that the Terrace Room was wonderfully convenient for the guest in a "hurry" and popular throughout the long cocktail hour. The Golden Lion (fourth from top) advertised, "The spirit of a robust age, England's empire building era, is reflected in this outstanding specialty restaurant. East-Indian-garbed waiters attend your every wish while master chefs prepare exotic flaming entrees. . . a specialty of the house." (Author's collection.)

GOOD MORNING THE OLYMPIC MENU. Featured here is a 1950s Olympic Hotel breakfast menu; Tom Gildersleve was the hotel's managing director. At this time, the Olympic was a Western Hotel. The menu featured a wonderful caricature of the Olympic Hotel smiling in a gold color on a red background to match the decor. (Author's collection.)

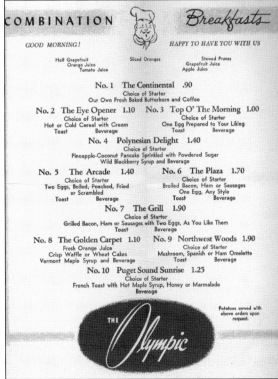

INSIDE GOOD MORNING MENU. On the menu were such dishes as creamed chipped beef on toast with beverage for $1.65, or a Puget Sound Sunrise, which included a choice of starter (fruit or juice), French toast, and beverage for $1.25. One of the most expensive breakfast entrees was Northwest Woods for $1.90. This meal included a choice of starter; a mushroom, Spanish, or ham omelet; toast; and a beverage. (Author's collection.)

THE OLYMPIC GRILL ROOM MENU. The grill was open from 6:30 a.m. to 1:00 a.m. and served a full menu. After one of the many remodels of the Olympic Hotel, retail space would take the place of the Golden Lion and the Olympic Grill. (Author's collection.)

OLYMPIC GRILL ROOM MENU INSIDE. Interesting items on the menu include the finnan haddie fleurette for $1, royal squab for $1.75, golden buck for 85¢, Scotch woodcock for $1, honeycomb tripe creole for 50¢, smoked fillets of imported bloaters for 35¢, and pickled tongue for 30¢. (Author's collection.)

We Call Your Attention

OYSTERS and CLAMS (to order)
Little Neck Clams on Half Shell 40
EASTERN BLUE OR TOKE {On Half Shell—Cocktail or Mignonnette Sauce 80
POINT OYSTERS {Baked in Shell, Any Style 1.00
(By Direct Shipment {Milk Stew 80   Half and Half 90   Cream Stew 1.00
OLYMPIA OYSTERS
In their own Juice 65   Fried 60   In Patty Shell, Poulette Sauce 1.00
Pancake with Bacon 1.00   Fancy Pan Roast 65   Milk Stew 65
Half and Half 75   Cream Stew 80

HORS D'OEUVRE (to order)
Crab Flakes, Salmon Flakes, Olympia Oysters or Shrimp Cocktail 40
Cracked Crab Mayonnaise 45   Half Avocado Vinaigrette 50
Crab Legs Cocktail 65   Crab Ravigote 50   Crab Louis 75 (all legs 1.00)
Marinated Celery Puget Sound with Crab Flakes or Shrimps 50

SOUPS (to order—served in bowls)
SPECIAL ONION SOUP AU GRATIN 35
Vegetable 20   Green Turtle with Sherry 50   Cream of Tomato 25   Split Pea 20
Consomme 15   Chicken Broth 25   Chicken Gumbo 25   Clam Broth 25

FISH (to order)
Clams Mariniere 45   Stuffed Baked Clams 45
Baked Fillets of Sole Bonne Femme 60   Grilled Salmon Maitre d'Hotel 65
Crab Flakes: Newburg 80, Deviled in Shell 60, Au Gratin 60   Crab Legs Brochette 80
Fried Fillets of Sole, Tartare Sauce 60   Rainbow Trout Meuniere 80
Jumbo Shrimps, Creole or Curry with Rice 75   Finnan Haddie Fleurette 1.00

FROM THE GRILL (to order)
(Garnished with French Fried Potatoes)
Pounded Steak 80   Steak Minute 1.00   New York Cut 1.50
Porterhouse Steak 2.00   T-Bone Steak 1.25   Fillet Mignon 1.75
Rump Steak 80   Hamburger Steak with or without Onions 45
Ham Steak 90   Pork Tenderloin 1.00   Calf's Liver and Bacon 70
Lamb Chop Mixed Grill 1.00   Lamb Chops (2) 1.00   Pork Chops (2) 1.00
Veal Chop (1) 80   Breast of Chicken with Virginia Ham 1.75
Squab Chicken 1.00   Half Spring Chicken 1.00   Royal Squab 1.75
Roast Lamb with Rib 60   Prime Ribs of Beef 65

ENTREES (to order)
Chili con Carne 50   Sliced Chicken a la King on Rice Pilaw, Glazed 85
Welsh Rarebit 80   Golden Buck 85   Scotch Woodcock 1.00
Home Made Noodles, Chicken Livers 50   Home Made Chicken Ravioli 50
Baked Pork and Beans 50   Honeycomb Tripe Creole 50

FRESH VEGETABLES (to order)
Brussels Sprouts 15   Creamed Puree of Celery Knobs 15   Baked Hubbard Squash 15
Peas 15   String Beans 15   Cauliflower 15   Artichoke 30   Zucchini 15
Corn on the Cob 15:- Saute 20   Lima Beans 20   Oyster Plant 15
French Fried Onions 20   Stewed Tomatoes 20   Grilled Tomatoes 15
Egg Plant 15   Broccoli 20   Young Carrots 10   Buttered Beets 10
Celery Milanaise 20   Small Onions in Cream 15   Creamed Spinach 10

POTATOES (to order)
Boiled 10   Lyonnaise 15   Mashed 15   French Fried 10   au Gratin 15
Cottage Fried 20   Rissolees 15   Julienne 10   Chips 10
Shoe String 15   Hashed Cream 15   Hashed Brown 15   Baked 20

SALADS (to order)
(Served with any kind of Dressing)
Cottage Cheese and Pineapple 30   Sliced Tomato 40   Potato 25
French Endive 50   Jumbo Asparagus 50   Asparagus Tips 40
Lettuce 20   Escarole 40   Romaine 40   Green Combination 40
Lettuce and Tomato 45   Fresh Cooked Vegetable Combination 45   Wilted Lettuce 40
Tuna Fish 65   Cole Slaw 30   Chef's Salad 40   Cosmopolitan 50
Fruit 60   Crab 65   Shrimp 65   Chicken 80   Waldorf 45

CHEESE (including rolls and butter)
New England 25   Home Made Cottage 15   Washington Double Cream 25
American 20   Domestic Swiss 25   Limburger 35   Old English 30
Imported Swiss 40   Roquefort 40   Imported English Cheddar 40   Edam 40
Oregon Cream 20   Pimento 25   Port du Salut 35   Liederkranz 45
Imported Stilton 40   Gorgonzola 40   Imported Camembert 40   Pimento 25

OLYMPIC HOTEL PALM TEA ROOM MENU. Shown here is the Olympic's Palm Tea Room menu. A chopped olive sandwich was 30¢, a cream cheese and walnut sandwich was 40¢, and a pate de foie gras (made of the liver of a specially fattened duck or goose) was 60¢. (Author's collection.)

The Olympic Hotel, Seattle
PALM TEA ROOM

OLYMPIC PALM TEA ROOM MENU INSIDE. On the inside of the Palm Tea menu were afternoon tea specials for 75¢ (not the $35 plus tax and tip that the Georgian Tea now charges). However, the author someday will gladly pay the $35 to enjoy tea sandwiches and homemade scones in such an elegant atmosphere. (Author's collection.)

Afternoon Tea, Special 75c

Orange Marmalade
Tea Biscuits
Dry or Cinnamon Toast
French Pastry or
Ice Cream and Cakes
Coffee, Chocolate
Tea

✦ ✦

Olympic Selected Teas and Coffee

English Breakfast   Oolong   Ceylon   Green
Orange Pekoe 25
Coffee 25
Ice Coffee with Whipped Cream 30
Chocolate or Cocoa with Whipped Cream 30

Afternoon Tea

✦

SANDWICHES
Chopped Olive 30   Chicken Salad 50   Chicken 50
Lettuce and Mayonnaise 30   Toasted Cheese 40
Cream Cheese and Walnut 40   Pate De Foie Gras 60

TOAST
Cinnamon Toast 15   Toasted English Muffins 15
Toast 15   Melba Toast 15   Zwieback 15
Raisin Bread Toast 15   Tea Biscuits 15

MARMALADE AND JAMS
Domestic Orange 20   English Dundee 35
Strawberry, Raspberry, Loganberry, Blackberry, Peach
or Pineapple Jam 30
Strained Honey 30   Bar le Duc 40

PASTRY
French Pastry 20   Fruit Tarts 20   Eclair 20
Fruit, Pound, Assorted Cakes 30
Petits Fours Glace 40

ICE CREAM
Vanilla 35   Chocolate 35   Strawberry 35   Pistachio 35
Parfaits—Strawberry 50   Cafe 50   Chocolate 50
Olympic 60   Coupe Jacques 60
Peach Melba 75   Strawberries Romanoff 75

SUNDAES
Pineapple 40   Chocolate Nut 40   Strawberry 50
Palm Court Special 75

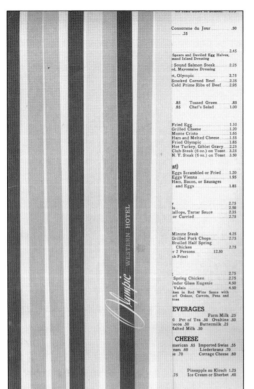

OLYMPIC WESTERN HOTEL MENU. Some interesting hors d'oeuvres listed on this menu were imported foie gras for $2.75, assorted tartines for $1.75, imported caviar on ice for $3.75, half fresh cracked crab for $1.75, and Olympia oyster cocktail for $3. (Author's collection.)

OLYMPIC WESTERN HOTEL MENU INSIDE. Other exciting menu items were Chateaubriand bouquetiere for two ($12.50), broiled rock lobster tails (2 for $2.75), and breast of capon under glass Eugenie ($4.50). (Author's collection.)

MENU

HORS d'OEUVRES

Half Grapefruit	.50	Assorted Tartines	1.75	Imported Caviar on Ice	3.75
Fresh Fruit Supreme	1.25	Assorted Canapes	1.75	Marinated Herring	
Avocado Pear	1.25	Smoked Salmon on Toast	1.25	in White Wine	1.25
Celery .50 Stuffed	.90	Crabmeat Cocktail Supreme	1.50	IN SEASON—	
Green Onions or Ripe Olives	.35	Crag Leg Cocktail Supreme	1.90	Half Fresh Cracked Crab	1.75
Spring Onions	.35	Shrimp Cocktail Supreme	1.50	½ Doz. Oysters	
Imported Foie-Gras	2.75	Olympia Oyster Cocktail	3.00	on Half Shell in Season	1.75

SOUPS

Soup du Jour	.50	Onion Soup au Gratin	.60	Consomme du Jour	.50
		Cold Madrilene .55	Cold Vichyssoise	.35	

FROM THE PANTRY

Maurice Salad Bowl	1.90	Trio Crab Salad	2.45
Julienne of Turkey and Ham, tossed with Crisp Lettuce and Maurice Dressing, Tomato Wedges		with Asparagus Spears and Deviled Egg Halves, Thousand Island Dressing	
Olympic Fruit Salad Plate	1.85	Cold, Fresh Puget Sound Salmon Steak	2.25
with Cottage Cheese or Sherbet Center		Garnished, Mayonnaise Dressing	
Fresh Crab or Shrimp Louis	2.45	Crab Legs Gourmet, Olympic	2.75
Thousand Island Dressing			
Cold Baked Ham	2.35	Cold Roast Turkey	2.35	Smoked Corned Beef	2.35
Smoked Beef Tongue	2.35	Assorted Cold Cuts	2.60	Cold Prime Ribs of Beef	2.95

DINNER SALADS

Lettuce and Tomato	.85	Romaine	.85	Hearts of Lettuce	.85	Tossed Green	.85
Asparagus Tips	.95	Potato	.75	Combination Vegetable	.85	Chef's Salad	1.00

SANDWICHES

Ham and Turkey	1.65	Tunafish	1.35	Fried Egg	1.10
Ham and Cheese	1.55	Crab Flake Salad	1.45	Grilled Cheese	1.20
Ham	1.25	Bacon, Lettuce and Tomato	1.10	Monte Cristo	1.65
Sliced Turkey	1.40	Ham and Swiss Cheese on		Ham and Melted Cheese	1.55
Chicken Salad	1.40	Olympic French Rolls (2)	1.55	Fried Olympic	1.85
Cold Roast Beef	1.90	Club House	1.90	Hot Turkey, Giblet Gravy	2.25
Olympic Special	1.65	Hamburger on a Bun	1.30	Club Steak (6 oz.) on Toast	3.25
Corned Beef	1.35	Ham or Bacon and Egg	1.55	N. Y. Steak (6 oz.) on Toast	3.50

EGG DISHES (Served with Toast)

Plain Omelet	1.35	Spanish Omelet	1.85	Eggs Scrambled or Fried	1.20
Minced Ham Omelet	1.95	Cheese Omelet	1.85	Eggs Vienna	1.95
Ham and Cheese Omelet	1.95	Poached Eggs on Toast	1.20	Ham, Bacon, or Sausages	
Chicken Liver Omelet	1.95	Eggs Benedict (2)	1.95	and Eggs	1.85

FISH

Butter Sauted Brook Trout, Belle Meuniere	2.50	Lobster Thermidor	2.75
Grilled Filet of Fresh Sole, Lemon Butter	2.35	Crab Legs St. Denis	2.50
Broiled Salmon Steak, Maitre d'Hotel	2.50	Fried Deep Sea Scallops, Tartar Sauce	2.35
Broiled Rock Lobster Tails (2)	2.75	Prawns Newburg or Curried	2.75

FROM THE GRILL

New York Cut Sirloin Steak,		Broiled Ground Sirloin		Minute Steak	4.25
Maitre d'Hotel (12 oz.)	5.50	Steak	2.50	Grilled Pork Chops	2.75
Filet Mignon	5.50	Broiled French Lamb Chops	4.50	Broiled Half Spring	
Club Steak	4.00	One Double Lamb Chop	2.00	Chicken	2.75
Broiled Ham Steak	3.25	Chateaubriand Bouquetiere for 2 Persons			12.50
(Above Items Are Garnished with Baked Potato or French Fries)			

ENTREES

Tournedos Rossini	6.50	Chicken a la King	2.75
New York Pepper Steak	5.50	Oven Baked Half Spring Chicken	2.75
Tenderloin of Beef a la Stroganoff	4.50	Breast of Capon Under Glass Eugenie	4.50
(Garnished with Egg Noodles)		Le Coq au Vin du Valais	
Calf's Liver and Bacon	3.50	Disjointed Chicken in Red Wine Sauce with	
Cutlet of Tender Veal a la Holstein	2.75	Mushrooms, Pearl Onions, Carrots, Peas and	
Veal Scallopini Parmigiana (with Spaghetti)	2.75	Parisienne Potatoes	

VEGETABLES

Tiny Whole Green Beans	.50	Carrots	.50
New Peas .50	Spinach	.50	Broccoli	.60
Green Asparagus .75	Pearl Onions in Cream	.55	

BEVERAGES

Pot of Coffee	.50	Farm Milk	.25
Instant Postum .50 Pot of Tea .50 Ovaltine	.50		
Chocolate or Cocoa	.50	Buttermilk	.25

Four

WHAT A RIDE!

Seattle, a little sleepy town of pioneers, was a quiet lumber town until 1884, when the railroad roared in and in 1897 the Alaskan gold rush Klondikers spent bags of money going back and forth to Alaska. Seattle suffered a disastrous fire in 1889, which burned down almost all hotels and restaurants in the entire central business district. Seattle quickly rebuilt out of brick.

During the Klondike gold rush, no one could go wrong in opening a hotel with a restaurant. The *Seattle Daily Times* August 6, 1897, issue reported, "More Klondikers than ever were in town last night. . . . For the first time since the firemen were walking the streets in the lower part of the city unable to get a bed, although they had money in plenty, the parlors in many of the hotels were filled with cots."

Seattle was booming with strangers at all hours of the day or night. That increased the need for restaurants, hotels, and other services. Prostitution was legal; gambling was legal; alcohol was legal; and morphine and opium were also legal. But whatever they did with the rest of their time, everyone in Seattle had to sleep and eat. Many of them did so at the 60-plus hotels built of brick after the fire of 1889, the workingman's hotels, or nearby restaurants. The well-to-do slept and ate at the fancier hotels like the famous Hotel Seattle (originally the Occidental) at First Avenue and Yesler Way, the Great Northern and Grand Pacific on First Avenue, or the Hotel Butler at James and Second Avenues. Some of them went bankrupt, but there were always entrepreneurs on the sidelines looking to find a good deal.

Remember Howard Bulson the talented piano man who played at the Firelite Room in the Moore Hotel? One could order a martini for 50¢ or a stinger for 60¢. Not in the mood for a drink? The Olympic Hotel's Palm Tea Room served an afternoon tea special for 75¢, which included orange marmalade, tea biscuits, cinnamon toast, and French pastry, or ice cream and cakes, coffee, chocolate, or tea. Enjoy this trip back through history.

OCCIDENTAL HOTEL. On September 26, 1881, memorial services for the assassinated president James A. Garfield were held at Occidental Square in front of the Occidental Hotel. The Occidental was located at the corner of James Street and Mill Street (later renamed Yesler Way) and Front Street (later renamed First Avenue). The Occidental was built in 1865 and demolished about 1883. (Courtesy Seattle Public Library 7292.)

FELKER HOUSE. Built in the late 1870s by Capt. Leonard Felker of the brig *Franklin Adams*, the Felker House was located out on Maynard's Point, near the corner of Railroad Avenue and Jackson Street. Mary Ann Conklin ran a brothel in the upstairs of the hotel, and it became known as "Mother Damnable's" or "The Conklin House." (Courtesy Clarence Bagley.)

ARLINGTON HOUSE. This photograph shows the Arlington House decorated for the visit of Pres. Benjamin Harrison on May 6, 1891. The Arlington was located at First Avenue South and Main Street near the Felker Hotel. (Courtesy Seattle Public Library 5172.)

NEW ENGLAND HOTEL. This photograph, taken by Peterson and Brothers around 1884, shows the intersection of Commercial Street (now First Avenue South) and Main Street looking north towards Mill Street (now Yesler Way). The New England House was on the left. Other signs in the photograph, from left to right, read: Miner's Supplies, Beer Hall, Stoves and Tinware, Clothing, and the San Francisco Store. (Courtesy MOHAI SHS470.)

HOTEL BRUNSWICK. On Commercial Street between Washington Street and Main Street was the Hotel Brunswick built in 1879. The Brunswick was destroyed in the Great Seattle Fire on June 6, 1889. On December 26, 1885, C. B. Collins and Julous Howser requested on Hotel Brunswick letterhead that the city license bootblacks' stands to "keep boys from going around with boxes." (Courtesy Seattle Public Library 5072.)

HOTEL KALMAR. The Kalmar was a workingman's hotel built in 1881 at Sixth Avenue and James Street. Leonard Brand, the last manager of the Kalmar, and his sister Viola fondly remembered the James Street cable cars climbing First Hill. The Kalmar was demolished in 1962 to make way for the Seattle Tollway (Interstate 5). (Courtesy Seattle Public Library 20019.)

OCCIDENTAL HOTEL. The second Occidental Hotel covered the triangle of land at Front Street and James Street. The Occidental was designed by Portland architect Donald MacKay in 1882 in the Second Empire style and completed in 1884. It was a stuccoed brick building with a mansard roof and bay windows framed in elaborate cast-iron moldings. This photograph shows the Yesler-Leary block at left, Occidental Hotel center, and the Colman building on the right. (Courtesy Seattle Public Library 22966.)

OCCIDENTAL HOTEL RUINS. On June 6, 1889, the Occidental Hotel lay in ruins, destroyed in the Great Seattle Fire. Shown here is the West facade. Bertrand Collins in the *Seattle Times* wrote that during the fire, owner John Collins ordered his Chinese workers onto the roof with wet blankets, "beating out the showers of sparks coming from the north." (Courtesy Seattle Public Library 5173.)

HOTEL SEATTLE. This photograph of the Hotel Seattle exterior looks eastward in the Pioneer Square district. The hotel was located at the corner of James Street and Yesler Way. The building was known as the Occidental Block, and the Seattle Public Library was hosted out of the third floor until 1894. John Collins bought one-third interest in the Occidental Hotel in 1867, and in 1879, he razed it to build a second Occidental—only to have that burn down in the Great Seattle Fire of 1889. Undeterred, Collins built the triangular-shaped Hotel Seattle in 1890. By 1914, the hotel had become an office building, and by 1961, it was abandoned. In the winter of 1961, the contents were auctioned off, and the hotel was razed. A "sinking ship" parking garage took its place. Seattle cried, and in 1970, the Pioneer Square Historic District was created. (Courtesy UWSC WAR0374.)

Program of Music Seattle Hotel. Dated Monday September 20, 1909, this program of music at the Seattle Hotel Café featured the Royal Hungarian Orchestra of Budapest. The orchestra would also happily honor requests when possible. The Seattle Hotel Café was located at First Avenue and James Street. (Courtesy Kent and Sandy Renshaw.)

Lobby Seattle Hotel. The Seattle Hotel featured a triangular shape, and so did its lobby. The hotel was five stories high. Seattle hotels offered two plans to their guests: the American Plan (lodging plus meals) and the European Plan (lodging only). The New England and Arlington Hotels charged $1 per day, while the upscale Seattle Hotel charged a full $2 a day. (Courtesy Kent and Sandy Renshaw.)

PROGRAM *of* MUSIC *at the* Seattle Hotel Cafe

FIRST AVENUE AND JAMES STREET

Week Commencing
Monday, Sept. 20th
1909

Part I.

From 6:15 until 8:30 p. m.

1	March "Hail to the Spirit *of* Liberty"	Sousa
2	Waltz "Confidence"	Waldteufel
3	Latest Popular Selection	
4	Rhapsodie "Hungarian"	Farkas
5	Overture "William Tell"	Rossini
6	Sentimental "There Never was a Girl like You"	Alystine
7	Violin Solo	Selected
	(Mr. M. S. Karp)	
8	Selection "Mlle. Modiste"	Herbert
9	Spanish Valse "La Susanna"	Losey
10	Finale	Selected

Part II.

From 10:30 until 12:30 p. m.

1	March "Hungarian-Turkish"	Szabadi
2	Waltz "Tales from the Vienna Woods"	Strauss
3	Popular	Selected
4	Cymbolum Solo "Robert the Devil"	Meyerbeer
	(Mr. Lacy Dobronyi)	
5	Hungarian Melodies	Dauko
6	Overture "Poet *and* Peasant"	Suppe
7	Rag "Popularity"	Cohan
8	Valse Lento "Monte Cristo"	Kotler
9	Sentimental "My Rosary"	Nevin
10	Finale "Rodetsky"	Strauss

Requests will be rendered with pleasure when possible

Royal Hungarian Orchestra *of* BUDAPEST

MR. LACY DOBRONYI . . . *Manager*
MR. M. S. KARP . . . . . *Director*

LOBBY SEATTLE HOTEL SEATTLE

HOTEL SEATTLE. Here is a photograph of the Hotel Seattle, at the corner of James Street and Yesler Way, looking east. The hotel had 150 rooms. Edward Camano Cheasty founded Cheasty's Haberdashery, Inc., in 1888. Cheasty paid $1,000 per month rent for space located on the corner of the hotel. Clarence Bagley wrote of Cheasty, "He carried an extensive line of both men's and women's wearing apparel and had one of the leading establishments of this character on the Pacific coast. The policy of the house was ever an unassailable one, and the name of Cheasty stood in Seattle as a synonym for business integrity and enterprise." His slogan was, "If it's correct, Cheasty Has It. If Cheasty has it, it's correct." Unfortunately, the Seattle retail section kept moving northward. On June 12, 1914, at the age of 50, Cheasty committed suicide by jumping off the roof of a hotel in the new retail section of town. (Courtesy UWSC SEA1199.)

SEATTLE HOTEL BUFFET. The postcard above is of the buffet located in the Seattle Hotel, managed by Bill Bonham. The Seattle Hotel was located at First Avenue and Yesler Way. It was a grand hotel in Pioneer Square, which has since been replaced by the "Sinking Ship," a parking garage. (Courtesy Janey Elliott.)

HOTEL SEATTLE GRILL. The print on the front of this card describes the subject of this photograph as "a section of the Hotel Seattle Grill." This postcard was postmarked May 1913 and was sent to a Dorothy Tuckel. The correspondence states that the sender spent Sunday with the Kings coming up from Portland and did not leave Alki Point all day. (Author's collection.)

TOTEM POLE AND SEATTLE HOTEL. Directly behind the famous totem pole in Pioneer Square was the Seattle Hotel. Seattle businessmen stole the 60-foot totem pole from Fort Tongass, brought it back to Seattle, and erected it in Pioneer Square on October 18, 1899. R. D. McGillvery described what happened, "The Indians were all away fishing, except for one who stayed in his house and looked scared to death. We picked out the best looking totem pole. . . . I took a couple of sailors ashore and we chopped it down—just like you'd chop down a tree. It was too big to roll down the beach, so we sawed it in two." The *Seattle Post-Intelligencer* paid $500 to the Tlingit Tribe for the totem although they wanted $20,000. In 1938, the totem was destroyed by an arsonist. In 1940, it was replaced by another carving by the descendants of the original tribe. (Author's collection.)

BELL'S HOTEL. Situated at 2330 First Avenue (the intersection of First and Battery Streets) was Bell's Hotel (also called the Hotel Bellevue or the Bellevue House), photographed here in 1898. William Nathaniel Bell and his wife, Sarah Ann (Peter) Bell, were members of the original pioneers that landed at Alki in 1851. Pioneer William Bell's hotel survived the Great Seattle Fire and stood at this location from 1883 until 1937. (UWSC, Wilse102C.)

HOTEL ARLINGTON. This postcard mailed in 1912 shows the Hotel Arlington, located at 1215 First Avenue at University Street. The hotel was also known as the Gilmore and Kirkman Building, Gilmore's Block, or the Bay Building on North Front Street. The building was designed by Elmer Fisher in 1889. The Seattle Post Office was located in its corner storeroom. (Author's collection.)

RAINIER HOTEL. The Great Seattle Fire destroyed over a dozen hotels, and 63 hotels were quickly built to replace them in the four-year period after the fire. The Rainier Grand Hotel at Marion and First Streets and the Rainier Hotel, pictured here, served as Seattle's main tourist hotels. In 1892, Frank LaRoche took this photograph of the Rainier Hotel on Fifth Avenue between Marion and Columbia Streets. The King County Courthouse is the building in the background on the right at Seventh Avenue between Alder and Terrace Streets. The Rainier was a large, framed building high atop the residential and commercial districts. After 1893's Wall Street panic, the hotel's linens were transferred to the Rainier Grand on First Avenue, and the Rainier Hotel was converted into the Rainier Apartments. This hotel, although it looks grand here, was hammered together in 80 days with such poor workmanship that no one was sad it was torn down. It was never a financial success as it was too far away from the financial district, and it was razed in 1910. (Courtesy MOHAI SHS1315.)

HOTEL BUTLER. In 1875, Hillory Butler stipulated that any building to be erected on his land must bear his name in perpetuity. The Butler was one of Seattle's first elegant hotels, and even though it has long since been demolished, Butler's name is still borne by the Butler parking garage. Also still surviving from the Hotel Butler era is the mahogany bar that escaped the axes of Prohibition and was sold in 1953 to the Ship's Tavern in Kodiak, Alaska. (Courtesy Alan Peterson.)

HOTEL BUTLER TOOTHPICK HOLDER. Pictured here is a silver toothpick holder from the Hotel Butler. In the photograph is also a bronze key fob from the Busch Hotel. (Author's collection.)

HOTEL BUTLER. In 1894, the Butler Block was converted into the Butler Hotel. The Butler's Rose Room became famous during Prohibition. Liquor was not sold by the establishment, but it did miraculously appear on local tables. The Butler was known to sell a lot of "ginger ale." As *Seattlife* magazine reported in 1939, "It was all in the course of an evening's fun to have the Prohibition agents swoop in, seize partially concealed bottles of liquor from under the tables, perhaps arrest an employe [sic] or two, and then depart amid boos and not-too-subtle insults." But on November 14, 1927, that changed: As patrons were dancing to Vic Meyer's orchestra playing, "How Dry I Am," hundreds of patrons dumped their drinks and shattered their glasses when they realized a major raid was under way. Some 18 customers were arrested by federal agents, and the Rose Room was closed down for a year. The Butler never was the same. On September 5, 1933, the hotel closed—just three months before the repeal of Prohibition. Its contents were auctioned on January 15, 1934. (Courtesy Seattle Municipal Archives 47329.)

Hotel Butler Annex. The Hotel Butler Annex was located at the corner of Fourth Avenue and Marion Street. Carleton Gilbert was the manager of this hotel, which offered furnished outside rooms with hot and cold water and steam heat. Single rooms with board were offered at $45 to $60 per month. (Courtesy Gary McCallister.)

C. C. Calkins Hotel. This 1890 photograph by Asahel Curtis shows the Calkins Hotel on Mercer Island. The Queen Anne–style building had 24 guest rooms, a ballroom, deep porches, turrets, and fancy spindle work. The resort flourished for a few years but closed in 1893 during the national depression. It later served as a school, a sanatorium, and a boardinghouse before burning to the ground in 1908. (Courtesy MOHAI SHS2097.)

HOTEL DILLER. The postcard above shows the Hotel Diller, which opened on June 6, 1890, the first anniversary of Seattle's Great Fire. Leonard Diller, owner, built his hotel, located at First and University Streets, with bricks imported from Japan as the Puget Sound's brickyards could not keep up with the demand. Seven hotels sprang up on First Avenue north of Yesler Way to accommodate transient workers; the Diller attracted Olympia's legislative leaders. (Author's collection.)

HOTEL FULTON. This photograph, taken on May 16, 1916, at Jackson Street and Second Avenue South, shows the sign for the Hotel Fulton on the left. Notice the huge sign for Swift Laundry Soap. The Fulton Hotel was also known as the Fulton Inn and the Totem Distributing Company in the Pioneer Square District. (Courtesy Seattle Municipal Archives 12329.)

ROYAL HOTEL DEMOLITION. Here is a photograph taken on July 11, 1911, of the Royal Hotel demolition. The razing occurred on Lot 8, Block 38, CD Boren's Addition, in the Pioneer Square section of Seattle. (Courtesy Seattle Municipal Archives 52185.)

THE FRANCES DEMOLITION. The Francis was totally demolished on August 28, 1911. The razing occurred on Lots 5 and 8, Block 40, CD Boren's Addition, in the Pioneer Square section of Seattle. (Courtesy Seattle Municipal Archives 52189.)

SEATTLE HOTEL. This photograph of Pioneer Square was taken in 1896 from the waterfront looking up Yesler Way. The waterfront was closer to the Seattle Hotel before city engineers sluiced down the hills of Seattle and filled up the sound. The Seattle Hotel had many lives. (Courtesy Seattle Municipal Archives 29984.)

OLYMPIC HOTEL IN PIONEER SQUARE. This April 21, 1930, photograph shows the totem pole at Pioneer Square with the Olympic Hotel standing behind it. In 1907, the same Olympic Hotel building simply advertised "furnished rooms." Pioneer's totem pole has been a Seattle landmark since 1899, when the pole was stolen from the Tlingit village in Alaska. (Courtesy Seattle Municipal Archives 4060.)

OLYMPIC HOTEL IN PIONEER SQUARE. This photograph of Pioneer Square shows the old Olympic Hotel and Merchants Café in the background. The Yesler cable car route opened in the fall of 1889 and was the oldest cable car in the Northwest. The underground cables powered by steam engines were replaced in 1912 by electric motors. The Yesler cable car line ran until August 1940. (Courtesy Seattle Municipal Archives 111260.)

HOTEL COLUMBIA. According to Jerry Torell, this photograph comes from around 1903 and features his grandfather Frank Oscar Boeck and his grandmother Anna Boeck standing in the door with their four children, Felix (8), Lothar (6), Erna (3), and Elsa (Jerry's mother, 2.) Built in 1892, the Hotel Columbia, pictured here, was located at 4900 Rainier Avenue South, Columbia City, and is now Lottie's Lounge. (Courtesy Jerry Torell.)

HUNTING LODGE AND WOODLANDS HOTEL. This photograph taken in 1891 shows the Hunting Lodge at the left (Fremont Avenue) entrance of Woodland Park where Guy C. Phinney died in 1893 at age 42. The two small boys on the right of the road are Arthur and Walter Phinney with the Woodlands Hotel in the background. (Courtesy Seattle Municipal Archives 30710.)

WOODLANDS HOTEL. In 1887, Guy C. Phinney bought 342 acres of land for $10,000 and built an English-style estate. The property was named Woodland Park and included a hunting lodge, conservatory, promenade, formal gardens, a menagerie (zoo), and the Woodlands Hotel. Currently, the African Savanna exhibit is situated where the Woodlands Hotel once stood. (Courtesy Seattle Municipal Archives 30709.)

GREAT NORTHERN HOTEL. Located between South Washington Street and Yesler Way was the Great Northern Hotel, also known as the Terry Denny building. This photograph was taken in 1898 by Anders Beer Wilse. The Great Northern attracted sourdoughs (old-time miners) and cheeckakas (newbies) from Alaska. In 2000, the Terry Denny building was fully renovated with 48 deluxe loft apartments and 8,000 square feet of ground floor retail space. (Courtesy MOHAI 1988.33.209.)

HOTEL CURTIS (FORMERLY THE SEDNEY). This photograph shows the Hotel Curtis— previously the Hotel Sedney— located at 1314 Second Avenue. Located next door at 1316 Second Avenue was the Hoffman Cloak Suit Company. (UWSC, Hamilton Collection 3832.)

GRAND PACIFIC HOTEL. Built in 1898 at 1115–1117 First Avenue, the Grand Pacific Hotel opened under the name "First Avenue Hotel." It was one of many post-fire structures on First Avenue. In the 1902 Seattle directory, the hotel was advertised as first-class and newly refurbished. The architect's name is lost to history. The Richardsonian Romanesque building was made of brick and limestone and constructed partially to cater to the needs of Seattle's growing transient laborer population—a need exacerbated by the Klondike gold rush. In 1982, the Grand Pacific Hotel was added to the National Register of Historic Places. (Courtesy Pemco Webster and Sevens Collection MOHAI 1983.10.7752.)

HOTEL CECIL. This 1910 photograph was taken by Asahel Curtis and shows the Cecil Hotel built in 1900 located at 1001–1023 First Avenue. The architect was Max Umbrecht, and the construction was of brick, terra-cotta, and iron. In 1982, the Globe Building, Beebe Building, and Hotel Cecil were added to the National Register of Historic Places. The Hotel Cecil is now the Alexis Hotel of the Kimpton hotel chain. In the middle of the afternoon in 2003, a man walked into the Alexis Hotel and sauntered out with a $40,000 Chihully glass bowl. (Courtesy UWSC CUR714.)

HOTEL LINCOLN. This advertisement for the Hotel Lincoln states that the tourist hotel has the largest and finest hanging garden in the world. The Lincoln catered to middle-class gentility and was considered a family hotel. (Courtesy Dan Kerlee.)

HOTEL LINCOLN INTERIOR. Sculptures lined the walls of the Lincoln Hotel lobby in 1905. On June 30, 1909, well-known Seattle women participated in a reception for suffragists at Seattle's Hotel Lincoln. The *Seattle Sunday Times* had primed the ground for suffrage on June 27, 1909, with an illustration about the coming meeting: "Oh the women! They are coming to Seattle by the trainload this week!" (Author's collection.)

HOTEL LINCOLN ROOF GARDEN. Hotel manager Adelaide Blackwell directed that the pergola and rooftop garden be built atop the Hotel Lincoln. Blackwell had flower gardens put in as well as a lawn and vines to cover the pergola. Guests could have tea amidst the gardens with a spectacular view; the gardens were literally the talk of the town. (Courtesy Kent and Sandy Renshaw.)

VIEW FROM LINCOLN HOTEL. This postcard shows a view from the Lincoln Hotel looking towards Puget Sound. Across the bay is Alki, where Seattleites went camping and where the city's original pioneers landed. In the distance are the snowcapped Olympic Mountains. (Courtesy Dan Kerlee.)

LINCOLN HOTEL. This April 6, 1920, photograph shows the Lincoln Hotel (burned April 6 and 7) between Third and Fourth Avenues on the north side of Madison Street. Charles C. Terry and his wife bought the land in 1867 for $250. James A. Moore bought it next, and in 1899, Dr. Rufus P. Lincoln bought the land with a modern apartment building for $24,000. (Courtesy Seattle Municipal Archives 1748.)

HOTEL LINCOLN DESTROYED. Hundreds of witnesses saw Fred R. Hamilton and his 20-year-old daughter Grace leap to their deaths from the fifth floor of the seven-story Hotel Lincoln. Four guests and one fireman died in the April fire of 1920. Chief Stetson described the Lincoln as "little else than a seven story lumber yard with four brick walls around it." (Courtesy Seattle Municipal Archives 1747.)

Hotel Lincoln Destroyed. Frank A. Jacobs, a local Seattle photographer, discovered smoke billowing from the laundry room just after midnight. The fire had crept slowly through concealed spaces to the upper levels. Hotel guests were rescued with aerial and pompier ladders. The west wall collapsed into the alley, injuring four firefighters and killing one. Some 15 minutes later, the south wall collapsed into Madison Street. (Courtesy of Seattle Public Library 22927.)

Plaza Hotel. The Plaza Hotel stood at the intersection of Fourth Avenue and Westlake from the early 1900s until 1935. The hotel advertised that every room was an outside room and under management of the Georgian Hotel Company. It was demolished in 1935. (Author's collection.)

HOTEL DIXON. This photograph, dated approximately 1901, shows the Hotel Dixon. The Dixon was located at the cross streets of Fremont Avenue and Ewing Avenue. Seattle's Fremont neighborhood, northwest of Lake Union, began in the 1880s as a settlement around a sawmill, and grew to a town of 5,000 before it was annexed by Seattle in 1891. (Courtesy Seattle Public Library 15267.)

COLONIAL HOTEL. Photographer Webster and Stevens took this photograph depicting the Colonial Hotel in 1911. The hotel was built in 1901 and is located at 1119–1123 First Avenue. The architect was Max Umbrecht, and the construction was of brick, terra-cotta, and iron. In 1982, the Colonial Hotel was added to the National Register of Historic Places. (Courtesy Pemco Webster and Stevens Collection MOHAI 1983.10.6734.)

am enjoying myself at the Sea Side boarding this Hotel, we are going to Victoria some day soon the boat from Seattle. also going to Portland fair. hope you

THE STOCKADE HOTEL. Built in 1901 by Alfred A. Smith, the Stockade Hotel, located at Alki Point in a west Seattle neighborhood, was a fashionable gathering place for Seattle socialites. The Stockade Hotel's advertised itself as "one of the finest summer hotels in the Pacific Northwest." The *West Seattle Herald* of April 9, 1932, heralded an upcoming performance of the Scintillators: "That snappy little jazz orchestra that has been playing for the American Legion meetings will play for a dance at the Stockade Hotel at Alki Beach this Saturday evening. The public is invited." In 1936, the hotel was torn down. (Courtesy Alan Peterson.)

Scene on Second Ave., Showing Savoy Hotel. Seattle, Wash.

SAVOY HOTEL STREET SCENE. This postcard, postmarked May 24, 1910, captures a street scene on Second Avenue that includes the Savoy Hotel. The unknown sender of this postcard wrote, "Well Halley's comet didn't get us after all. We are having fine weather here. Saw a full eclipse of the moon and the comet. Wish you had been here. This country just suits me." The Savoy was imploded in September 1986. (Courtesy Connie Cody.)

Hotel Savoy, Seattle

HOTEL SAVOY. The Hotel Savoy at 1212–1216 Second Avenue dominates this postcard. The structure was first built as an eight-story hotel, and four floors were added later. In 1931, a man committed suicide by jumping out a hotel window. The following year, Savoy bellboys were arrested on rum-running charges. In 1945, a guest was crushed by an elevator. In 1966, prostitutes were arrested for working in the Nero Room. (Courtesy Mark Sundquist.)

HOTEL STEVENS. This 1916 postcard shows the Hotel Stevens, located on the corner of First Avenue and Marion Street (the George F. Fryes Block). The back of the card reads, "Rooms 75¢ per day and up. A first-class family place devoted particularly to local transient people." The Henry M. Jackson Federal Building takes up the entire block today. Arthur Denny (1822–1899) established Seattle's first post office in 1852 in this same location. (Author's collection.)

OTIS HOTEL. The Otis Hotel was located on Summit Avenue between Columbia and Marion Streets, now in the heart of the Swedish Medical Center. Both its location and appearance suggest a residential use. The Otis Hotel was built approximately 1905. Seattle historian Clarence Bagley wrote of a devastating fire at the Otis Hotel caused by "a lady using an alcohol lamp" on the morning of March 29, 1908. The loss was $10,655. (Author's collection.)

104675

MOORE HOTEL. Built in 1907 to cater to the guests of the Alaska-Yukon Pacific Exposition, the Moore Hotel advertised itself as "an exceptional Hotel at Moderate Rates." Located on Second Avenue at Virginia Street, it had 200 rooms, was fireproof, and sat at the center of the city's activities. The Moore Hotel was constructed of reinforced concrete, with white glazed brick cladding. (Author's collection.)

PACIFIC NORTHWEST
The Summer Playground of America

Part Lobby ~ MOORE HOTEL ~ SEATTLE

MOORE HOTEL EXTERIOR AND LOBBY. James A. Moore, an early Seattle real estate developer, built the Moore Hotel and Moore Theatre. The building was designed by Edwin W. Houghton and included marble and onyx in the theater and foyer. The building was listed on the National Register of Historic Places on August 30, 1974, and is still operating today. (Courtesy Kent and Sandy Renshaw.)

MOORE HOTEL FIRELITE ROOM MENU. Howard Bulson, a talented piano man, played at the Firelite Room. In 1954, Eddie Zollman entertained with his organ and piano music. James A. Moore built the Moore Hotel in conjunction with the Moore Theatre, currently Seattle's oldest entertainment venue. Both are still open at 1926 Second Avenue. (Author's collection.)

The Moore Hotel

MAin. 4851

1926 SECOND AVENUE   SEATTLE 1, WASHINGTON

FIRELITE ROOM DRINK MENU. People could toast their tootsies by the open fireplace in this cozy lounge adjacent to the Moore Hotel, 1920. The Firelite Room drink menu offered a Firelite Cocktail for 50¢ and an Alaska Cocktail for 60¢. Some of the drinks' names, like the Moscow Mule, make one wonder what was in them. (Author's collection.)

We will be pleased to serve your favorite drinks and liqueurs

Firelite Room

May We Suggest . . .

Firelite Cocktail	.50
Alaska Cocktail	.60
Canadian Cocktail	.60
Martini	.50
Manhattan	.50
Old Fashioned	.50
Rob Roy	.65
Daiquiri	.50
Frozen Daiquiri	.60
Bacardi	.50
Stinger	.60

COOL DRINKS

Tom Collins	.50
Rum Collins	.50
Gin Fizz	.50
Silver Fizz	.60
Golden Fizz	.60
Royal Fizz	.60
Singapore Sling	.75
Whiskey Sour	.50
Planter's Punch	.75
Moscow Mule	.60

Blended Whiskey	.50
Straight	.60
Bonded	.70
Scotch, 6 Year Old	.60
Canadian	.60
Beer, Western .25; Eastern	.30
Wine	.40

For Room Service . . . Add 10c

PHOTO BY NOWELL & ROGNON.

A Scene at the Public Market,
First Avenue and Peke Street, Seattle.

HOTEL LELAND. This postcard image, taken in 1913 at the Seattle Pike Place Market, shows the Hotel Leland built in the late 19th century. Brothers Frank and John Goodwin of Goodwin Real Estate owned the Leland in 1907. Can you imagine a $10-a-month room at the Leland? (Courtesy Mark Sundquist.)

HOTEL LELAND ROOM. This 1972 photograph shows a typical room at the Hotel Leland. *Seattle Times* reporter Don Duncan had painful memories of the Leland Hotel: "My maternal grandfather, Robert Metz, lived there in a cramped little room with an iron bedstead, a hotplate, a sink, and a single light bulb that hung from the ceiling on a long cord." (Courtesy Seattle Municipal Archives 32434.)

HOTEL ELLIOTT AND HOTEL LELAND. Looking west down Pike Street in 1910 with the Hotel Elliott (Hahn Building, 1908) on the left of the street and the Hotel Leland on the right, this image captures the early days of the Pike Place Market. On April 8, 1973, the Hotel Leland's furnishings were auctioned off at the market. (Courtesy Seattle Municipal Archives 33278.)

OUTLOOK OR LASALLE HOTEL. The Outlook Hotel was built in 1908 at the Public Market (Pike Place). After the attack on Pearl Harbor, many Japanese and Japanese American–owned businesses at the market were ruined as persons of Japanese descent were forced into internment camps. Nellie Curtis took over a Japanese American family's lease on the Outlook Hotel, renamed it the LaSalle Hotel, and ran a lucrative brothel there until 1951. (Courtesy Seattle Municipal Archives 35919.)

SORRENTO HOTEL. The Sorrento Hotel, 1908, is shown under construction at the northwest corner of Madison Street and Terry Avenue on lower First Hill in Seattle. The hotel was designed by architect Harlan Thomas, who on a visit to Europe, fell in love with Italian villas. Named after Sorrento, Italy, the hotel was owned by clothing merchant Samuel Rosenberg. (Courtesy Sorrento Hotel.)

SORRENTO HOTEL. This postcard shows the Hotel Sorrento in about 1912. A new circular drive has replaced the small formal garden shown here. Fr. Francis Corkery, SJ, president of Seattle College (now Seattle University), in 1938 leased an entire wing of the Sorrento as a women's dormitory. Rosenberg traded the Sorrento for Bear Creek Orchards, which his sons turned into the multimillion-dollar enterprise David and Harry. (Author's collection.)

SORRENTO STOCK CERTIFICATE. Shares for the Sorrento Hotel. dated February 1, 1915, sold for $100 each. This Sorrento stock certificate lists V. F. Pavey, a successful real estate entrepreneur and attorney. Several publications and articles listed Pavey as the proprietor and owner of the Sorrento, but tax records show Samuel Rosenberg, Bear Creek Orchards, and/ or the Rosenberg estate still listed as the owner. (Courtesy Sorrento Hotel.)

SORRENTO FIRESIDE ROOM. A softly colored Mediterranean landscape painted on the Italian tile above the wood-burning fireplace still greets guests at the Sorrento. Honduras mahogany paneling adorns the room. At one time, the famous Air Force Base—a lounge in the lobby—was a gathering place for hundreds of U.S. Air Force personnel. Visiting U.S. Air Force men would sign their names to currency from around the world and tack it to the ceiling—though this tradition began after the time of this photograph. (Courtesy Sorrento Hotel.)

SORRENTO HOTEL TEA ROOM. This photograph was taken about 1921 of the Sorrento Hotel Tea Room. When the Sorrento opened in 1909, President Taft came to dedicate the Alaska-Yukon-Pacific Exposition and was one of the first guests to sign the register. Taft rode in the brass-door lift (elevator), and to this day, this original elevator remains the only elevator of the hotel. If elevators could talk. (Courtesy Sorrento Hotel.)

SORRENTO HOTEL DINING ROOM. This photograph shows the Sorrento Dining Room about 1921. The Sorrento advertised itself as "a hotel in the heart of things." The Top O' the Town, Seattle's first rooftop restaurant, was legendary for more than 70 years, with its rooftop garden amid spectacular views of Elliott Bay, Puget Sound, and the Olympic Peninsula. The dining room became a banquet facility. (Courtesy Sorrento Hotel.)

TOP O' THE TOWN MENU. The Sorrento Hotel's Top O' the Town restaurant was once a popular entertainment spot serving its famous roast beef dinner. Inside the menu was a bit of history and Native American legend on the rhododendron, Washington's state flower. (Author's collection.)

TOP O' THE TOWN MENU. This menu from Top O' Town featured prime rib of Eastern steer beef carved at the table. Included was a baked potato with all the trimmings, fresh vegetables, garlic French bread, a choice of dessert, and a beverage—all for $4.75. In 1954, Merceedes Welcker, radio and television star, appeared nightly. (Author's collection.)

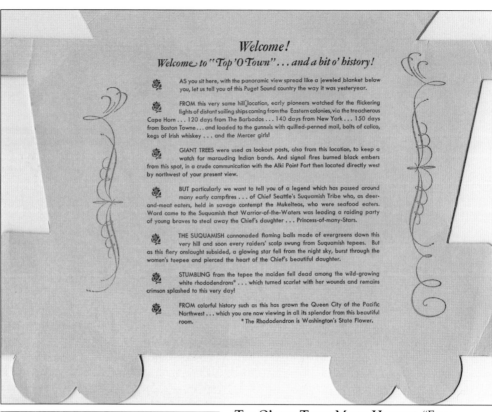

Welcome!

Welcome to "Top 'O Town" . . . and a bit o' history!

AS you sit here, with the panoramic view spread like a jeweled blanket below you, let us tell you of this Puget Sound country the way it was yesteryear.

FROM this very same hill location, early pioneers watched for the flickering lights of distant sailing ships coming from the Eastern colonies, via the treacherous Cape Horn . . . 120 days from The Barbados . . . 140 days from New York . . . 150 days from Boston Towne . . . and loaded to the gunnels with quilled-penned mail, bolts of calico, kegs of Irish whiskey . . . and the Mercer girls!

GIANT TREES were used as lookout posts, also from this location, to keep a watch for marauding Indian bands. And signal fires burned black embers from this spot, in a crude communication with the Alki Point Fort then located directly west by northwest of your present view.

BUT particularly we want to tell you of a legend which has passed around many early campfires . . . of Chief Seattle's Suquamish Tribe who, as deer-and-meat eaters, held in savage contempt the Mukelteos, who were seafood eaters. Word came to the Suquamish that Warrior-of-the-Waters was leading a raiding party of young braves to steal away the Chief's daughter . . . Princess-of-many-Stars.

THE SUQUAMISH cannonaded flaming balls made of evergreens down this very hill and soon every raiders' scalp swung from Suquamish tepees. But as this fiery onslaught subsided, a glowing star fell from the night sky, burst through the women's teepee and pierced the heart of the Chief's beautiful daughter.

STUMBLING from the tepee the maiden fell dead among the wild-growing white rhododendrons* . . . which turned scarlet with her wounds and remains crimson splashed to this very day!

FROM colorful history such as this has grown the Queen City of the Pacific Northwest . . . which you are now viewing in all its splendor from this beautiful room.   * The Rhododendron is Washington's State Flower.

TOP O' THE TOWN MENU HISTORY. "From this very same hill location, early pioneers watched for the flickering lights of distant sailing ships coming from the Eastern colonies, via the treacherous Cape Horn . . . 120 days from the Barbados . . . 140 days from New York . . . 150 days from Boston Towne . . . and loaded to the gunnels with quilled-penned mail, bolts of calico, kegs of Irish whiskey . . . and the Mercer girls!" (Author's collection.)

HOTEL GEORGIAN. This postcard of Fourth Avenue looking south shows the Hotel Georgian on the left side of the street. Built in 1908, the Georgian had seven stories and 108 rooms. The building was made of brick veneer and reinforced concrete. In 1963, Peoples Bank bought the hotel building for $365,000 from Charles B. Steele. (Courtesy Dan Kerlee.)

COMMODORE HOTEL. This postcard shows the Commodore Hotel, located at 2013 Second Avenue and built in 1909. The hotel had all outside rooms with an excellent view of the city when it was built. (Courtesy Alan Peterson.)

HOTEL SEWARD. Seattle is shown at night looking up Third Avenue; the Hotel Seward, built in 1909, is the building on the left. The upscale Hotel Seward later became the Morrison Hotel. The second story of the building was taken by the Arctic Club, making the Seward "one of the most important business structures in the city," according to *Alaska Yukon Magazine* in 1909. (Courtesy Mark Sundquist.)

SEATTLE AT NIGHT. LOOKING UP THIRD AVENUE.

HOTEL RHEIN. Depicted here is a 1914 postcard of the Hotel Rhein that was located at Eighth Avenue and Union Street. In 1910, the Rhein advertised rates of $3 to $5 a week with "special monthly rates." Several local schoolteachers lived there. An advertisement reads: "Clean House in every respect. Elegant café in connection" W. M. Haitz was the manager. (Author's collection.)

REHAN HOTEL. This postcard of the Rehan Hotel, located at Eighth Avenue and Union Street, shows the hotel when Paul Kambic was the manager. Patrons could come to the Seattle World's Fair and only pay $5 for a room with a detached bath or $7.50 for an in-room bath. Later the Rehan Hotel was razed to make way for the Seattle Convention Center. (Author's collection.)

Seattle's HOTEL MORRISON
509—3rd Ave., opp. County-City Bldg.

300 Comfortable
Outside Rooms
With Baths

HOTEL MORRISON. Located at 501 Third Avenue in Pioneer Square was the Hotel Morrison (originally the Arctic Club and Hotel Seward), built in 1909. The Alaskan window appears on the first floor of the Morrison. Notice that the top of the Smith Tower has been doctored out of this postcard. Historylink.org reported that the Caper Club, located in the Hotel Morrison, offered dancing with live and recorded music to a predominately gay clientele. In 1966, police officers from the Seattle Police Department forced the club to pay $165 a week in protection money. A June 1970 trial exposed these practices and led to convictions, forced resignations, and a complete reorganization of the Seattle Police Department. Currently the building is being used for transitional housing and a shelter, and it still has its share of problems. (Courtesy Nancy Hoppe.)

ALKI POINT SUMMER RESORT. This postcard was postmarked June 2, 1910. Alki Point catered to Seattle's influential and was an area of vacation homes and resorts. Alki Beach is the site of the landing of the first white settlers in Seattle on a cold and rainy November 13, 1851, and was originally named New York Alki. (Author's collection.)

Partial View of Lobby, Hotel St. Regis, Seattle.

HOTEL ST. REGIS LOBBY. This partial view of the lobby shows the high ceilings, a marble staircase with a 6-foot marble pillar at the base of the staircase, and the ornamental cast iron and brass railing. The carpeting protected an Italian terrazzo floor. The mocha-colored brick building was located at the northwest corner of Second Avenue and Stewart Street. The building was constructed in 1909 as the Hotel Archibald. Now called Plymouth on Stewart, the hotel has been turned into apartments that house the homeless. (Courtesy Gary McCallister.)

CALHOUN HOTEL. Scott Calhoun built the Calhoun Hotel for $125,000 in 1909–1910 at the corner of Second Avenue and Virginia Street. Designed by architect William P. White, it was the tallest building north of Virginia Street and the first modern block erected in the Denny Hill regrade. (Author's collection.)

CAFÉ OF NEW CALHOUN HOTEL. This 1913 postcard shows the café of the New Calhoun Hotel. The Calhoun had eight floors with 152 rooms and was built in six months. Plans for the basement included a rathskeller (a beer tavern below street level). (Courtesy Mark Sundquist.)

TRIANGLE HOTEL AND BAR (FLATIRON). Architect C. A. Breitung designed and built the Triangle Hotel in 1910, having been inspired by New York City's Flatiron Building. This December 12, 1910, photograph was taken by James P. Lee as he was looking north from First Avenue South and Railroad Avenue, showing the Flatiron Building at 551 First Avenue South. In 1976, the Triangle Hotel and Bar was added to the National Register of Historic Places. (Courtesy UWSC, LEE169.)

NEW RICHMOND HOTEL POSTCARD. Built for R. C. McCormick, the New Richmond Hotel was located at 501 1/2 South Main Street at the Fourth Avenue South corner of South Main Street. The hotel promoted itself as "The Most Homelike Hotel in City," but still "Close to Everything Worth While." The hotel brochure assured potential guests that the beautiful new 10-story building was "absolutely fireproof." (Author's collection.)

New Richmond Hotel, Seattle, Wash.

AMERICAN HOTEL. This photograph of the American Hotel was taken by Webster and Stevens in 1911. The original American Hotel was destroyed on July 26, 1879, but a new one rose in its place. A document found in the Seattle Municipal Archives states: "March 30, 1894, Louis Gnecchi filed a claim for damages and loss of property caused to his business 'American Hotel' during a quarantine. The Committee on Claims recommended that he be paid only for items destroyed by City officials and not for the loss of business during the quarantine." (Courtesy Pemco Webster and Stevens Collection MOHAI 1983.10.6635.)

RIGHT HOTEL. The Right Hotel was located at the southeast corner of Columbia Street and First Avenue, the site of the first school in Seattle (1854). An office building named the Sullivan Block later replaced the school. Sievert W. Thurston came to Seattle as a member of the Icelander team of acrobats. Harold Maltby and Thurston bought the building and turned it into a hotel. The partners had founded a group called Western Hotels, and this was their first hotel venture together. Thurston later became head of Western International Hotels. The address was 712 First Avenue in Seattle's central business district. This *c.* 1923 photograph was taken by an unidentified photographer. In 1957, the Bank of California acquired the Right Hotel and the building was razed and replaced by—you guessed it—another high-rise parking garage. (Courtesy UWSC SEA1535.)

FRYE HOTEL. This photograph by Asahel Curtis looks southeast from Yesler Way around 1925. When the Frye was built, it was one of the highest of the city's new steel-frame brick and terra-cotta tile skyscrapers. Advertisements suggested, "When in Seattle Try the Frye." (Courtesy Seattle Public Library 22635.)

FRYE HOTEL. On April 6, 1911, the Hotel Frye made its debut. George Frye, age 70, personally supervised the construction of the 340-room, 11-story elegant Italian Renaissance Louisa C. Frye Hotel (named after his wife). The U.S. Navy took over the Frye during World War II. In 1955, the Frye was a motor hotel, and in 1971, it became a low-rent apartment complex. (Courtesy John Cooper.)

HOTEL FRYE
3rd Avenue at Yesler Way
SEATTLE, WASHINGTON

IN THE HEART OF THE EVERGREEN PLAYGROUND

FRYE HOTEL. The building has an H-shaped plan with a primary entrance on Yesler Way and another one on Third Avenue South. The Frye Hotel had entertainment and dancing nightly in the Rose Room, which featured excellent cuisine and music. The Frye was located opposite City Hall Park and the county-city buildings. (Courtesy Kent and Sandy Renshaw.)

FRYE HOTEL, 1940. This August 9, 1940, photograph of Yesler Way captures the streetcar's last day in operation. Taken at Third Avenue and Yesler Way, the image also shows the Frye Hotel. George and wife Louisa (Denny) Frye also built and managed at least three other hotels, built the Frye Opera House, and owned a successful meatpacking company and bakery. (Courtesy Seattle Municipal Archives 39626.)

FRYE HOTEL ADVERTISEMENT. Located at Third Avenue and Yesler Way, the Frye was designed by Charles Herbert Bebb and Louis Leonard Mendel. Dan W. Bass and P. H. Watt were the hotel's managers. "We have pleased half a million guests in four years' time and can please you," boasted hotel literature. Recently, the Low Income Housing Institute purchased the hotel and restored the main floor. (Author's collection.)

THE ALLEN HOTEL. This photograph, taken by Seattle's Engineering Department on August 20, 1911, shows the back of the Allen Hotel. The entrance was around the corner on Yesler Way. Rooms cost $1–$2 per week. Housekeeping rooms went for $2–$4 per week. Thus, lodging cost a mere 15¢–50¢ per day. (Courtesy Seattle Municipal Archives 52187.)

HOTEL RECTOR. In May 1913, the Hotel Rector opened at Third Avenue and Cherry Street. The building was designed by Seattle architect John Graham, and the contractor was Harry Brandt, who built the hotel for Alson Lennon Brown. The Rector had 105 rooms and was six stories high, although the original architectural plans called for a nine-story building. The Rector was built in the Beaux-Arts style, incorporating Beaux-Arts and American Renaissance motifs. Architect Herbert B. Pearce designed the storefronts, which were built by J. Levinson, who became the hotel's general manager and owner after it opened. The grand entrance from the marble stair landing in the Rector Hotel's lobby opened directly to the balcony of the Grand Opera House Theater. In 1918, the hotel became the Hotel St. Charles and in 1999 was turned into a low-income apartment building by the Plymouth Housing Group. (Notice the Smith Tower under construction behind the hotel in this postcard.) (Author's collection.)

CITY HALL AND COURT HOUSE

6A-H2762

HOTEL HOLLAND. Built opposite the new courthouse, the Holland Hotel was fireproof. It was a well-known and popular hostelry, where a guest could enjoy comfort and refinement at attractive rates. The Holland was located at Fourth Avenue on the northeast corner of Jefferson Street. It was built around 1912. (Courtesy Mark Sundquist.)

HOTEL BADEN. The Hotel Baden was located at First Avenue and Pine Street. The publisher of this postcard was Edward H. Mitchell. (Author's collection.)

ROSS SHIRE HOTEL. This June 24, 1914, photograph shows the Ross Shire Hotel located at Sixth and Marion Street during the Sixth Avenue regrade. This picture shows a bit of Seattle's gratuitous regrading. The Ross Shire Hotel was also known as Ross Shire Apartments, and there was a Ross Shire Café. (Courtesy Seattle Municipal Archives 2386.)

RAINIER GRAND HOTEL. This postcard shows the Rainier Grand Hotel, built by the Noyes family of Butte, Montana. It was located at 909–915 First Avenue, between Madison and Marion Streets. In the 1930s, the U.S. government bought the entire block and built the Federal Office Building. (Author's collection.)

RAINIER GRAND HOTEL SOAP DISH. Here is an amazing soap dish from the Rainier Grand Hotel with an image of Mount Rainier towering over Puget Sound. This dish was found in the ground by Mark Sundquist at a local ghost town. (Author's collection.)

"Halibut Fishing," one of the Paintings in the Famous Collection in the Parlors of Rainier-Grand Hotel, Seattle, U. S. A.

HALIBUT FISHING. Halibut Fishing was one of the paintings in the famous collection in the Rainier Grand Hotel's parlors. The Rainier Grand was also known for its bar, which featured a variety of Manhattan cocktails dubbed "Nector for Ye Gods." On September 11, 1908, inventor Thomas A. Edison (1847–1931) stayed at this hotel with his wife and daughter. (Author's collection.)

Hotel Raleigh, 1408 Fourth Ave., Seattle, Wash.

HOTEL RALEIGH. This postcard shows the Hotel Raleigh, located at 1408 Fourth Avenue. (Courtesy Bill Mix.)

HOTEL YOROZOYA. This photograph was taken January 16, 1915, and shows several Japanese-owned businesses such as the K. Kumata Company, Tailor; the Hotel Yorozoya; and the Yokohama Laundry. Seattle has always suffered from slides and the one in this photograph was on Main Street at the intersection of the west margin of Maynard Avenue, looking east. The slide extended about 9 feet. (Courtesy Seattle Municipal Archives 50669.)

Arctic Building. In 1908, an Arctic Club was formed in Seattle. This photograph was taken by Webster and Stevens in 1919 of the Arctic Building. Arctic Club members commissioned A. Warren Gould in 1916 to design the Arctic Building at 306 Cherry Street. Originally the Arctic Club was located at Third Avenue and Jefferson Street. Boys will be boys: when the Arctic Club relocated, several members stole their original bar by hoisting it out the window. Soon afterwards, it miraculously turned up at the new building pictured here. No less than 27 terra-cotta walrus heads adorned the exterior of the third floor. Originally the walrus tusks were made of ivory. Congressman Marion Anthony Zioncheck (1901–1936), while up for re-election, jumped from the window of his campaign office in the Arctic Building and fell to his death on August 7, 1936. The Arctic Building was listed in the National Register of Historic Places in 1978 and has been reborn as the Arctic Club Hotel. (Courtesy Pemco Webster and Stevens Collection MOHAI 1983.10.10417.)

SECOND AVENUE HOTELS. Several hotels line Second Avenue just north of Yesler Way in this 1920 photograph. Starting from left to right are the Hotel Milburn, the Fourth Avenue Hotel, the Hotel Reynolds, and the Grand Union Hotel. (Courtesy Seattle Municipal Archives 46549.)

THE KENNETH HOTEL. One of Seattle's biggest heists occurred over the weekend of February 20–22, 1954, when burglars broke into Pioneer Safe Deposit Vaults located in the basement of the Kenneth Hotel. On that Saturday, local law enforcement officers were attending a 60th annual Police Ball. The burglars got off with between $200,000 and $500,000, and they were never caught. The Kenneth was razed in 1968 for another parking garage. (Courtesy Mark Sundquist.)

THE WALDORF HOTEL. The postcard featured here shows the Waldorf Hotel and its new parlor lobby sometime around 1921. The hotel was located on the northeast corner of Seventh Avenue and Pike Street and built by the General Engineering Construction Company. It was demolished for the development of the Washington Trade Center. (Courtesy Kent and Sandy Renshaw.)

CORNER NEW PARLOR LOBBY

There's a little hotel at Seventh and Pike
The kind of a spot that's easy to like
And it makes no difference how far you roam
This same little place reminds you of home.

Always a welcome, the latch string is out
Frank, king of bell boys is somewhere about.
Across the old desk with your key in his hand
Stands smiling sheik Sam the best in the land.

A voice from behind says "Hello there old
    Friend"   [mend.
And believe me your blues are sure on the
Somehow the walls, the ferns and the birds
Bring to you music and a song without words.

The head of this house like a wonderful dad
To him all his children are good, never bad.
The kindliest smile in those two eyes of brown
A laugh of good cheer and never a frown.

'Tis midnight now and I am writing along
The fault let me say is entirely my own,
For down in the lobby the Kerosene Club
Can make a good man out of merely a dub.
                                            [had
Perhaps it's the ghost of a dream-home you've
There's something that's different and makes
    you feel glad
In this little hotel at Seventh and Pike,
It's the sort of spot that's easy to like.

WALDORF HOTEL, SEATTLE.
7TH AND PIKE.

WALDORF HOTEL INK BLOTTER. This ink blotter lists Elmer L. Gibson as the vice president/treasurer and Dolph S. Edmiston as the manager of the Waldorf Hotel. Of course, after the Great Seattle Fire, every hotel in Seattle advertised that it was fireproof. In 1954, the Oaken Bucket was a quiet, rustic rock-walled garden atmosphere cocktail lounge, complete with oaken bucket stools. (Courtesy Gary McCallister.)

One of Seattle's Most Popular Hotels Announces

A New Deal

300 Rooms   Free Garage   Fireproof

NOW You can enjoy a comfortable
Room with Bath $1.50
F O R   O N L Y

Or a Large, Well Furnished Room $1.00
With Detached Bath for

Take advantage of this new deal and
HAVE THE DIFFERENCE TO SPEND

Elmer L. Gibson
Vice-Pres. - Treasurer

Dolph S. Edmiston
MANAGER

Waldorf Hotel
One of Seattle's Largest Down Town Hotels
7th at PIKE   -   SEATTLE

Hotel Barker,
Pike St. and Sixth Ave.

Absolutely Mode
Seattle, Wash.

CLAREMONT APARTMENT HOTEL

BILL CORBETT
OWNER AND MANAGER

MAIN 8600
FOURTH AND VIRGINIA
SEATTLE

HOTEL BARKER. This postcard shows the Hotel Barker located at 518 Pike Street. An advertisement in the *Issaquah Press* on May 5, 1922, advertised "Courteous treatment to your Wife, Daughter, Mother and Sister. Center of Shopping and Theater Districts. Corner of Sixth and Pike . . . All outside rooms. Rooms $1.50 and up. Bath $2 and up; Garage in connection." (Courtesy Bill Mix.)

CLAREMONT APARTMENT HOTEL. The Claremont Apartment Hotel at Fourth Avenue and Virginia Street was a popular post-Denny regrade residential hotel built in 1925 by Stephen Berg. In 1954, the Clef Room was part of Seattle's newest supper club. Bill Corbett, owner and manager, was indicted November 14, 1956, for willful evasion of income tax. Located in the Belltown district, it is currently named the Hotel Andra. (Courtesy Alan Peterson.)

Cornelius Apartment Hotel. This linen postcard from the 1940s shows the Cornelius Apartment Hotel, located at 306 Blanchard Street in the Belltown area of Seattle. Built in 1925 by architect Frank Fowler for owner Carroll Cornelius, the hotel was notable for the pink tile cladding on its first two stories. The back of this postcard advertises, "Some of Seattle's finest Transient Rooms," which was appropriate for Seattle's booming population. (Courtesy Alan Peterson.)

CORNELIUS APARTMENT HOTEL

Third and Blanchard   SEATTLE, WASH.

Vance Hotel, Seattle, Washington

Vance Hotel. Built in 1926, The Vance Hotel was mainly clad in buff brick and terra-cotta. The back of the postcard states, "The Vance Hotel is located at 7th and Stewart Streets, Seattle 1, Wash. The 'Friendly' hotel located one block from the Central Bus Depot and convenient to the downtown shopping, theatrical and business district. Comfortable rooms and excellent food at reasonable prices." (Courtesy Evelyn Marshall.)

111

CAMLIN HOTEL. This is a 1926 Webster and Stevens photograph of the Camlin Apartment Hotel. The Camlin was located at 1619 Ninth Street and the architect was Carl Linde, who built the edifice to resemble an Italian castle in the Tudor Revival style. The latest amenities included dinettes and kitchenettes and shower baths in the 93 apartments. The 11th floor was a penthouse. In 1942, the unsuccessful penthouse was converted into the very successful Cloud Room restaurant. The Cloud Room offered a grand view of Seattle through huge windows and an outdoor terrace. In 1999, the Camlin Hotel was added to the National Register of Historic Places. In 2003, Trendwest Resorts bought the building, and during remodeling, 40 kitchenettes that were walled up in 1949 were uncovered, featuring their original 1924 Hotpoint Automatic Electric Stoves worth several thousand dollars each. (Courtesy Pemco Webster and Stevens Collection MOHAI 1983.10.3408.1.)

HOTEL NORWAY AND HOTEL PALMER. This photograph from Seattle's Department of Streets and Sewers is dated August 24, 1927. It shows the Hotel Norway on the left and the Hotel Palmer on the right. The men in the image were placing Amiesite asphalt at Seventh Avenue South and Dearborn Street. No other photographs of these two hotels could be located. (Courtesy Seattle Municipal Archives 38263.)

THE NEW HOTEL HUNGERFORD. The corner of Fourth Avenue at Spring Street has been a busy corner. Herman and Katherine Bagley built a Victorian home in the 1880s on this corner; it was torn down in 1903, and James McNaught built a larger mansion on the same spot. In 1928, the ultra-modern New Hotel Hungerford replaced the McNaught mansion. Earl Hungerford was the owner and manager of the New Hotel Hungerford, shown here. The hotel later became the Pacific Plaza Hotel, which is now the Executive Hotel Pacific. (Courtesy Kent and Sandy Renshaw.)

BENJAMIN FRANKLIN HOTEL. Built in 1929, the Benjamin Franklin Hotel was Seattle's second-largest hotel. The Benjamin was 14 stories high with 359 rooms. It was designed by Gardner J. Gwinn and operated by the Benjamin Franklin Hotel Company. The Benjamin was hit by the wrecking ball in July 1980. Betty Bowen, whose life centered around the Benjamin Franklin as its public relations person, would have said, "Bye, Love." (Courtesy Kent and Sandy Renshaw.)

BENJAMIN FRANKLIN HOTEL LOBBY. Margaret Reed's father was a doorman at the Benjamin and wore a uniform like Benjamin Franklin. Bill Hulett was another doorman at the Benjamin; he later became vice president of Western International Hotels. The hotel's cashier, Gordon Bass, became president of Western International. (Courtesy Alan Peterson.)

OUTRIGGER IN BENJAMIN FRANKLIN HOTEL. The photograph shown here is of the world-famous Outrigger, created by Trader Vic, in the Benjamin Franklin Hotel. Here a waitress serves customers in September 1959. The Outrigger was renowned for its authentic setting and unusual food. The Benjamin Franklin Hotel was located at Fifth Avenue and Virginia Street. (Courtesy *Seattle Post-Intelligencer* Collection, MOHAI 1986.5.11383.1.)

NEW RICHELIEU HOTEL. This photograph was shot on January 26, 1929, as Seattle was doing some brick repaving on Third Avenue, north towards Marion Street. Other identifiable business signs in the image are those for Shorey's Book Store, the Traders Building, and the Oxford Tailoring Company. (Courtesy Seattle Municipal Archives 3252.)

ROOSEVELT HOTEL. Built in 1929 at Seventh Avenue and Pine Street during the Great Depression, the Roosevelt Hotel still has its pink neon rooftop sign lit 24 hours a day. The hotel was named after Pres. Theodore Roosevelt. There are five commissioned national parks oil paintings throughout the hotel. Historic Von's Restaurant is now called Von's RoastHouse and Martini Manhattan Memorial and is currently located in the Roosevelt Hotel. (Courtesy Evelyn Marshall.)

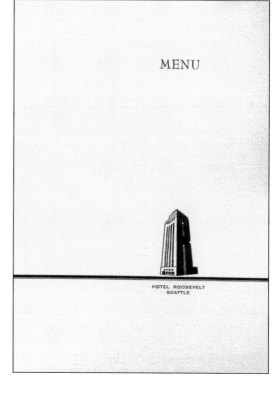

ROOSEVELT HOTEL MENU. This menu from the Roosevelt Hotel is dated Friday 19, 1940. The hotel offered a Roosevelt corned beef hash deluxe with fresh vegetable salad, hot rolls, and coffee for 40¢. (Author's collection.)

Roosevelt Hotel Menu Inside. The hotel restaurant featured a southern pan-fried chicken dinner for $1, which included a Dungeness crab cocktail, lettuce and tomato salad, and pan-fried chicken ("jointed heavy colored fryers fried in the old fashioned way in butter in a pan until crisp and golden brown") served with creamy gravy, sweet potato, and new green peas. (Author's collection.)

Von's Restaurant. On Easter, March 29, 1959, Von's Rabbit approaches a family dining at Von's Restaurant, offering candy. Von's Restaurant takes its name from restaurateur John G. von Herberg. Von's Restaurant, located in the Roosevelt Hotel at Pine Street and Seventh Avenue, is still in operation. (Courtesy Robert H. Miller Collection, MOHAI, No. 2002.46.26.)

Roosevelt Hotel, Seattle

SOUTHERN PAN FRIED CHICKEN DINNER $1.00
Dungeness Crab Leg Cocktail
Lettuce and Tomato Salad, French Dressing
Pan Fried Chicken (Jointed Heavy Colored Fryers Fried in the Old Fashioned Way in Butter in a Pan until Crisp and Golden Brown) Served with Creamy Gravy and Sweet Potato and New Green Peas
Hot Rolls   Butter   Coffee

Friday, July 19, 1940

De Luxe Dinner

(Served from 5 to 9 p. m.)

Assorted Relishes

Fresh Olympia Oyster Cocktail		Grape, Orange Cup	
Chilled Watermelon		Apple Juice	
Sea-food Bisque		Clam Chowder	

	Complete Dinner	Du Jour Dinner
Broiled Tenderloin Steak	1.25	1.00
of Blue Ribbon Steer Beef Served with French Fried Potatoes, Corn on the Cob		
Grilled Calf's Liver, Spiced Apricot	1.00	75
Whipped Potatoes, Corn on the Cob		
Broiled Club Steak	1.10	85
Marinated in Sherry Wine and Imported Olive Oil, Served with Whipped Potatoes, French Fried Egg Plant		
Baked Stuffed King Salmon	90	70
Mushroom Sauce, Browned New Potatoes, Buttered Peas and Carrots		
Breaded Veal Cutlet, Tart Jelly	85	65
French Fried Shoestring Potatoes, New Peas in Butter		
Roast Shoulder of Pork	85	65
Cinnamon Apple Ring, Whipped Potatoes, Summer Squash in Butter		
Shirred Eggs with Pig Sausages	75	55
Baked Together in Casserole, French Fried Shoestring Potatoes		
Spanish Steak	75	55
Whipped Potatoes, French Fried Egg Plant		
Chicken Timbale	65	55
Garnished with Slices of Hard Cooked Eggs, Whipped Potatoes, Buttered Beets		

Tomato Aspic Ring Filled with Crisp Celery

DESSERTS

Hot or Cold Apple Pie   Cocoanut Cream Pie   Lemon Soufflé Pudding
Hot Fudge Sundae   Fresh Strawberry Crepe
Fresh Pineapple Sundae   Baked Washington Apple
Cocoanut Apricot Bombe   Sliced Raw Apple with Cheese
Pineapple Bombe   Fresh Strawberry or Butterscotch Rum Sundae
Ice Cream   Sherbet   Cup Custard   Jell-O, Whipped Cream
Bartlett Pears   Pineapple Tidbits   Home Style Peaches
Edam, Old English, Camembert or Leiderkrantz Cheese and Crackers
Corona Coffee   Tea   Grade A Milk

55c DINNER
Rolled Roast of Lamb, Gravy
Browned New Potatoes, Buttered Beets
Hot Rolls   Coffee, Tea or Milk

ROUGH RIDER ROOM LOUNGE. Written on the back of this postcard was the following: "The Rough Rider Room is one of the Northwest's most distinctive Lounges. A new touch of The Old West gives The Utmost in Comfort and Relaxation." (Author's collection.)

TOURIST HOTEL. This photograph was taken November 30, 1949, of earthquake damage at the Tourist Hotel, located at Main Street and Occidental Avenue. The Tourist Hotel was later named the Palmer House. In 1980, the name was the Rainbow Hotel—but there was no gold at the end of the Rainbow. On October 11, 1980, the hotel was razed for a parking lot. (Courtesy Seattle Municipal Archives 41826.)

HOTEL ALBANY. Standing on Third Avenue looking north from Marion, this street scene photograph was taken April 21, 1930, and pictures the Hotel Albany. Notice the sign on the hotel advertising modern rooms for $1. Other signs advertise the Oxford Tailoring Company, Raymer's Books, the Pacific Coast China Company, and the Cozy Lunch. (Courtesy Seattle Municipal Archives 4060.)

HOTEL LIVINGSTON. Hotel Livingston and Livingston Café are pictured here at A. A. Denny's on Sixth Street, block 37, lot 2 (undivided 1/2) on First Avenue. The photograph was taken by the King County Assessor sometime between 1931 and 1937. (Courtesy Seattle Municipal Archives 31839.)

BED ROOM

AMBASSADOR HOTEL, SEATTLE, WASH.

AMBASSADOR HOTEL. This postcard shows the Ambassador Hotel, where both R. Marshall and Walter G. Bovee served as managers. In 1935, the hotel unwittingly became involved in a famous FBI case, the Weyerhaeuser kidnapping. George H. Weyerhaeuser, age nine, was kidnapped on May 24, 1935, from Tacoma. His captors demanded $200,000 and instructed the boy's father, lumber magnate J. P. Weyerhaeuser Jr., to register at 7:00 p.m. at the Ambassador Hotel, 806 Union Street, and expect instructions. The ransom was paid and young George Weyerhaeuser was released at a shack near Issaquah, Washington, on June 1, 1935. The boy wandered into the home of the Bonifas family, where he was fed and driven towards home. The FBI and local police unleashed what many remember as "the greatest manhunt in the history of the Northwest." Weyerhaeuser's captors were caught and sentenced to prison, and $157,319.47 of the ransom money was returned. Daryl C. McClary on historylink.org reported, "After the case in appreciation for helping his son, J. P. Weyerhaeuser Jr. gave Louis Bonifas lifetime employment in the Weyerhaeuser Timber Company's Snoqualmie Falls Lumber Mill, and a monetary reward of sufficient size to purchase several acres of land and build a new house in the Snoqualmie area. Young George Weyerhaeuser ultimately grew up to become Chairman of the Board for the Weyerhaeuser Company." (Courtesy Kent and Sandy Renshaw.)

Fish from your window

Edgewater Inn, Seattle

EDGEWATER INN. Since 1962, the Edgewater has occupied Pier 67 on the site of the former Galbraith Bacon Pier. Originally it was named the Camelot, then the Edgewater Inn; it is currently named the Edgewater Hotel. In 1964, the Beatles, after their first world tour, stayed at the Edgewater. Other Seattle hotels rejected the Beatles as guests, but the Edgewater gladly accepted them even though the hotel had to install cyclone fencing around the hotel to keep the screaming fans from rushing the band. The Beatles fished from the window of room 272. In 1969, Led Zeppelin stayed in Seattle's Edgewater Inn and the infamous "mudshark incident" transpired. In June 1971, the "Mud Shark" was immortalized in song by Frank Zappa during a Fillmore East gig. Other musical groups and celebrities that stayed at the Edgewater were KISS, the Rolling Stones, Frank Zappa, Ozzy Osbourne, the Village People, Jewel, Neil Young, Wings, Blondie, and Pearl Jam. (Author's collection.)

EDMOND MEANY HOTEL. A 1930s postcard of the Edmund Meany Hotel, located in the University District is seen at left. Named after Professor Meany, the hotel's grand opening was held on November 11, 1931. Designed by architect Robert C. Reamer, the Edmond Meany Hotel became a center of University District activities. The building is a remarkable example of the art deco style. In 1986, the hotel was reopened as the Meany Tower Hotel and, after a $2 million renovation, is now the Hotel Deca, decorated in a contemporary art deco motif. (Courtesy Alan Peterson.)

HARBORVIEW HOTEL. Located at 1605–1609 1/2 First Avenue was the Harborview Hotel and Hansen's Café. The photograph was taken about 1937. (Courtesy Seattle Municipal Archives 31921.)

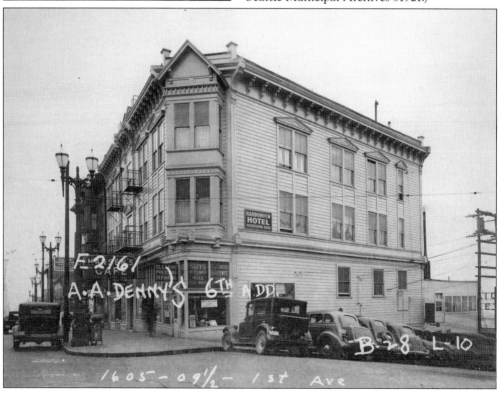

REGENCY HYATT HOUSE.
The Hyatt House opened in
1960 and was the hip place
to party in SeaTac. Famous
guests included Johnny Cash,
the Rolling Stones, Tina
Turner, and Sly and the Family
Stone. The Hyatt was the
setting for the 1965 film *The
Slender Thread*, starring Sidney
Poitier and Anne Bancroft.
In 1989, the Hyatt became
the Radisson, which closed in
2006. (Author's collection.)

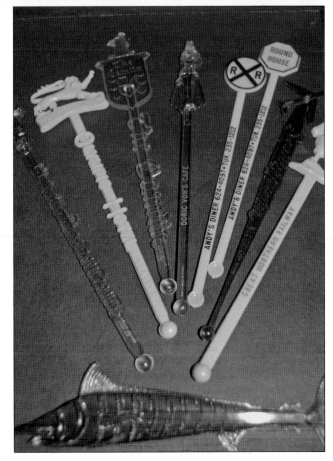

SWIZZLE STICKS. Assorted
Seattle hotel swizzle sticks
are pictured here. From left
to right, they come from
Clarks Restaurants, Golden
Lion (Olympic Hotel), the
Camlin (Sorrento), Doric
Von's Café, Andy's Diner, the
Seattle–Tacoma Airport, and
the Great Northern Railway.
(Author's collection.)

THE COLLINS HOT SPRINGS HOTEL. This postcard comes from the Collins Hot Mineral Springs Hotel, located in Collins, Washington. The state of Washington has 30 hot springs; the Collins Hot Springs was located in The Dalles. Its waters averaged 122 degrees Fahrenheit. (Author's collection.)

ST. MARTIN HOT SPRINGS HOTEL. This postcard comes from the St Martin's Hot Springs, located in Carson. Carson Hot Springs were discovered in 1876 near the Columbia Gorge by Isadore St. Martin. The St. Martin Hotel was completed in 1901, and the bathhouse and cabins were added in 1923. Carson Hot Springs Resort and its healing waters are still open to the public. (Author's collection.)

"See Washington First." Mount Rainier from Longmire Springs. The building in the foreground is the Hotel Longmire.

HOTEL LONGMIRE. The text on the postcard urges tourists to "See Washington First." The photograph shows Mount Rainier from Longmire Springs. The building in the foreground is the Hotel Longmire. In 1883, James Longmire built a trail to the hot springs and by 1906 had built the 30-room Longmire Springs Hotel. In 1987, the Longmire Buildings were declared a National Historic Landmark. (Author's collection.)

BARNESTON HOTEL. This photograph, taken on March 19, 1911, shows the Barneston Hotel. The company mill town of Barneston, established in 1898, was one of three towns in the Cedar River Shed (near Carnation) that were forced into oblivion; Cedar Falls and Taylor also got the boot. In 1910, the population of Barneston was 156. The last person left town on December 31, 1923. Barneston's buildings were demolished in 1924. (Courtesy Seattle Municipal Archives 48053.)

INDEX

www.arcadiapublishing.com

Discover books about the town where you grew up, the cities where your friends and families live, the town where your parents met, or even that retirement spot you've been dreaming about. Our Web site provides history lovers with exclusive deals, advanced notification about new titles, e-mail alerts of author events, and much more.

MADE IN THE USA

Arcadia Publishing, the leading local history publisher in the United States, is committed to making history accessible and meaningful through publishing books that celebrate and preserve the heritage of America's people and places. Consistent with our mission to preserve history on a local level, this book was printed in South Carolina on American-made paper and manufactured entirely in the United States.

This book carries the accredited Forest Stewardship Council (FSC) label and is printed on 100 percent FSC-certified paper. Products carrying the FSC label are independently certified to assure consumers that they come from forests that are managed to meet the social, economic, and ecological needs of present and future generations.

FSC
Mixed Sources
Product group from well-managed forests and other controlled sources

Cert no. SW-COC-001530
www.fsc.org
© 1996 Forest Stewardship Council

Find Your Place in History.